WONDER WOMAN

Ends of the Earth

Gail Simone
Writer

Aaron Lopresti & Matt Ryan (#20-23)
Bernard Chang (#24-25)
Artists

Brad Anderson
Kanila Tripp
Colorists

Travis Lanham
Steve Wands
Letterers

Wonder Woman created by
William Moulton Marston

Dan DiDio
Senior VP-Executive Editor

Matt Idelson
Editor-original series

Nachie Castro
Associate Editor-original series

Anton Kawasaki
Editor-collected edition

Robbin Brosterman
Senior Art Director

Paul Levitz
President & Publisher

Georg Brewer
VP-Design & DC Direct Creative

Richard Bruning
Senior VP-Creative Director

Patrick Caldon
Executive VP-Finance & Operations

Chris Caramalis
VP-Finance

John Cunningham
VP-Marketing

Terri Cunningham
VP-Managing Editor

Amy Genkins
Senior VP-Business & Legal Affairs

Alison Gill
VP-Manufacturing

David Hyde
VP-Publicity

Hank Kanalz
VP-General Manager, WildStorm

Jim Lee
Editorial Director-WildStorm

Gregory Noveck
Senior VP-Creative Affairs

Sue Pohja
VP-Book Trade Sales

Steve Rotterdam
Senior VP-Sales & Marketing

Cheryl Rubin
Senior VP-Brand Management

Alysse Soll
VP-Advertising & Custom Publishing

Jeff Trojan
VP-Business Development, DC Direct

Bob Wayne
VP-Sales

Cover by Aaron Lopresti with
Alex Sinclair
Logo design by Nancy Ogami

WONDER WOMAN:
ENDS OF THE EARTH

DC Comics, 1700 Broadway,
New York, NY 10019
A Warner Bros. Entertainment
Company
Printed in USA. First Printing.

ISBN: 978-1-4012-2136-2
SC ISBN: 978-1-4012-2137-9

WONDER WOMAN #20
Cover by Aaron Lopresti with Alex Sinclair

I'M TOLD THE WEATHER IS LIKE THIS MOST OF THE YEAR.
I MISS THE TROPICS, TRUTH BE TOLD.
THE JEALOUS COLD WANTS TO CLAIM THE BREATH FROM MY LUNGS. I CAN NO LONGER FEEL MY LEGS OR ARMS. I'M HERE ON THE WHIM OF A MADMAN.
AND THERE IS MORE...
...I AM BEING HUNTED.

I'M NEAR. I CAN SMELL THE WOODFIRE.
BUT THE BEASTS ARE STARVING. AND DESPERATE.

THEY'RE SUMMONING THEIR COURAGE.
AND I HAVEN'T MY POWERS HERE.

THE MEAD HALL.

HUH. THE WOLVES. HUNGRY AND DESPERATE THEY MAY BE.

BUT ONE THING MORE, AS WELL...

ENDS OF THE EARTH
Part 1 of 4
AN UNREASONING FROS
...THEY'RE CLEVER.

UHNN.
THEY'RE...
...THEY'RE BEYOND EVEN ANIMAL REASON.
THEY HAVE NO FEAR, ONLY RAGE.
LOATH AS I AM TO KILL ANIMALS...
...THERE MAY BE NO CHOICE.
NO CHOICE AT ALL.
HUNTERS OF THE CLAW AND FANG, I BESEECH THEE. DO NOT DIE THIS NIGHT.
GO.
LEAVE!

THEY SHOULD HAVE RUN BY NOW.
UNLESS...
THANKFULLY, MY LASSO REMAINS TRUE.
PEACE.
DREAM OF FIELDS OF EASY PREY, WOLF LORDS.
IT'S AS I FEARED.

DISEASE.
THEY'VE LOST TOUCH WITH THEIR INSTINCTS.
THEY'RE DYING.
RAGE THIRST HATE PAIN SICKNESS HATE HUNGER THIRST PAIN PAIN PAIN PAIN
PEACE, HUNTER.
IT WON'T BE LONG NOW.
THE LASSO SOOTHES THEM, MOMENTARILY. BUT OTHERWISE, THEY KNOW NOTHING BUT AGONY AND FEAR.
THEY'RE BEGGING FOR RELEASE, BEFORE THEY LOSE THEIR WAY AND TURN ON EACH OTHER.
A PACK, TO THE END.
I HEAR YOU, TRACKER. THE GIFT OF HEPHAESTUS HEARS YOU.
FORGIVE ME.
AND THEN THE DEED IS DONE.
MAY YOURS BE THE LAST INNOCENT BLOOD SHED TODAY.
THIS IS THE PRECISE TIME AND LOCATION WHERE HE SHOULD BE ARRIVING.
I'VE COME SOME FAIR DISTANCE. MAY MY INFORMATION BE ON TARGET.

THE MEAD HALL.
A CIVILIZED RETREAT, WHERE EVEN OPPOSING SOLDIERS COULD SHARE IN COMPANIONABLE FELLOWSHIP, IN RESPITE FROM WAR AND FAMINE.
<SO, AND THIS IS THE GOOD BIT, HE REACHES OUT AND HE BASHES THE MAN'S SKULL IN, RIGHT? AND WE'RE ALL LAUGHING, BECAUSE OF THE SOUND IT MAKES, A LITTLE POP SOUND, IF YOU WILL...>
<...AND AGAIN, WE'RE LAUGHING, WHEN THE FELLOW'S CAPTAIN COMES UP, AND SAYS, WHAT ARE YOU LOT WAITING FOR? LIKE WE'RE SUPPOSED TO FIGHT THIS THING, RIGHT?>
THE INNKEEPER ORDERS ME TO LEAVE. SAYS HE DOESN'T WANT MY KIND HERE.
I BELIEVE HE'S MISREAD MY PROFESSION.
<AND I SAY, "WHY, GOOD CAPTAIN, WHY NOT GO AND TALK TO HIM YOURSELF, AS WE'RE JUST WAITIN' TO HEAR THAT QUEER LITTLE NOISE AGAIN!">
AND MY RESOLVE.
HA HA HA HA! HA HA HA HA HA! HA HA HA HA! HA HA HA!
AND NOW I WAIT.

TURNS OUT MY INFORMATION WAS ON THE MARK.
<I SEEK THE SPAWN OF CAIN.>
<DESCENDANT OF THE FIRST MURDERER.>
<I KNOW HE CAME THIS WAY. WHERE IS HE? WHERE IS THE DEMON?>
HE'S HERE. IT'S REALLY HIM.
BEOWULF.
<YOU WILL ANSWER ME, RABBLE. I AM KING HROOGAR'S SWORD-ARM!>
<WHERE. IS.>
<GRENDEL?>

DEPARTMENT OF METAHUMAN AFFFAIRS, SIX SHORT HOURS AGO...
JUST A ROUTINE PERFORMANCE EVALUATION, AGENT PRINCE. NOTHING TO BE NERVOUS ABOUT.

ARE YOU NERVOUS, AGENT PRINCE?
NOT AT ALL, DIRECTOR STEEL.

WHY IS THAT, I WONDER?
PERFECTLY NORMAL HUMAN REACTION TO FEEL ANXIETY AT A TIME LIKE THIS.

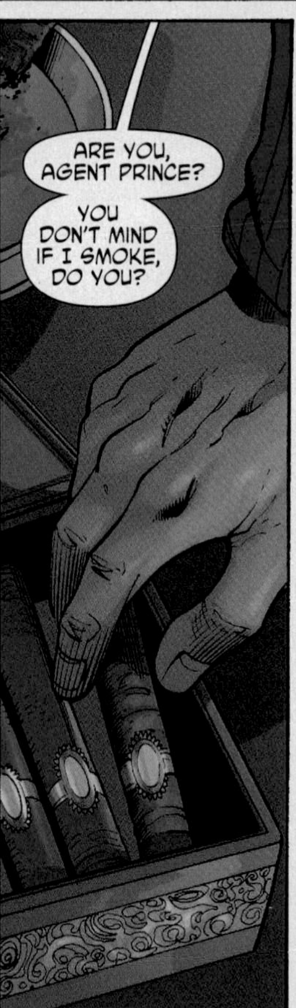
ARE YOU, AGENT PRINCE?
YOU DON'T MIND IF I SMOKE, DO YOU?

AM I WHAT, DIRECTOR?
I DO. AND IT'S ILLEGAL IN A GOVERNMENT OFFICE.

PERFECT.
NORMAL.
HUMAN.
JUST PICK ONE, I GUESS.

HOW DID YOU SURVIVE BEING ATTACKED BY CAPTAIN NAZI, AGENT PRINCE?
HOW DID YOU MANAGE TO LIVE THROUGH BEING IN THE MIDDLE OF A C-4 DETONATION?
I'M EVER SO CURIOUS.
TRAINING, SKILL AND LUCK, DIRECTOR. ANOTHER TIME, I MIGHT NOT BE SO FORTUNATE.
IF YOU HAVE NO FURTHER BUSINESS?
I DO, ACTUALLY.
I'M PROMOTING YOU TO SENIOR FIELD AGENT.
YOU WILL ASSEMBLE A TEAM OF SIX, UNDER YOUR COMMAND, FROM THESE PROSPECTS I CHERRY-PICKED MYSELF.
CHOOSE WISELY. YOUR LIFE DEPENDS ON IT.
BUT...
YOU ARE DISMISSED, AGENT PRINCE. CONGRATULATIONS.
BUT...
DISMISSED.
BUT...
SLAMMMM

COMMISSARY, NOW, AGENT PRINCE.
AND FOR PETE'S SAKES, CLOSE YOUR MOUTH, PLEASE.
MY CLOSEST FRIEND, AND MOST TRUSTED ADVISOR OUTSIDE OF THEMYSCIRA, ETTA CANDY.

SHE CLEARLY HAS SECRETS SHE'S NOT READY TO TELL ME YET. SHE'S EARNED THAT.
TODAYS SPECIAL
PEPPERED LOAF
4.99
SO? WHAT'D OL' SALTY DOG HAVE TO SAY?
HE PROMOTED ME.
BUT, BUT THAT'S GREAT!
IS IT?

HE'S JOUSTING WITH ME, KEEPING ME OFF GUARD. IT'S A WARRIOR'S TACTIC, NOT A REWARD FOR ACHIEVEMENT.
MAYBE. OR MAYBE YOU'RE PARANOID. HAVE YOU CONSIDERED USING THE, YOU KNOW, THE LITTLE GOLDEN POLYGRAPH ON HIM?
THE LASSO OF TRUTH?
WOULD YOU USE A NUCLEAR BOMB TO KILL A MOUSE?

MAYBE. BUT I REALLY HATE MICE.
THIS THING IS GROTESQUE. WHAT IS A PEPPERED LOAF?
VEGETARIANISM SAYS I NEEDN'T ANSWER THAT.

FAIR ENOUGH. BUT PEOPLE ARE GOING TO WANT ANSWERS, DIANA.
LET ME ASK YOU THIS, GIRLFRIEND TO GIRLFRIEND...
...WHY DID YOU TAKE THIS JOB?

I DO NOT LIE. I BELIEVE IN THE TRUTH.
BUT SOME TRUTHS ARE A HYDRA, WITH PRECIOUS FEW OF THE HEADS REVEALED.
IT'S...
IT'S A DISCONNECTEDNESS. A FEELING OF REMOVAL.

I WANT TO KNOW YOUR SOCIETY, ETTA. I HAVE TRIED.
IT'S HARDER THAN I THOUGHT.
JUST PROMISE ME YOU WON'T GO BACK TO SLINGING NACHOS AT THAT FAST FOOD JOINT.
BECAUSE SHE'S MY FRIEND, SHE DOESN'T PRESS.

AND, AS IS THE AMERICAN CUSTOM, WE LAUGH OFF OUR MOMENTARY AWKWARDNESS.
WELL, YOU HAVE TO ADMIT, THE UNIFORMS ARE BETTER HERE THAN AT TACO WHIZ.
I LIKED THE LITTLE HAT.
YES. HATS ARE...
...HATS ARE GOOD.
USING BANTER TO AVOID THE TRUTH.
BUT IT'S A QUESTION THAT DESERVES A PROPER ANSWER. AND SOON.
WELL, SINCE I'M PRYING, I HAVE ANOTHER QUESTION FOR YOU.
IT'S ABOUT THE MEN IN YOUR...

...OFFICE?
HELLO, LADIES.
DON'T LET ME INTERRUPT.

AN INTRUDER? HERE? IN MY OFFICE?
THAT'S THE GUY I TOLD YOU ABOUT, FROM YOUR APARTMENT!
HANDS UP, SCUZZBALL!
DIANA PRINCE
SOMEDAY, ETTA. I VOW.

I REALLY MUST TEACH YOU HOW TO ADDRESS AN ENEMY PROPERLY.
HEY!

HOW COULD HE GET PAST THE BEST SECURITY SYSTEM IN THE COUNTRY? AND MORE IMPORTANTLY...
...HOW DID I NOT SENSE HIS PRESENCE?
I COULD KILL YOU FOR THAT, YOU KNOW.
I MOST CERTAINLY COULD.

I THINK NOT.

I'LL WANT THAT BACK, AGENT PRINCE.

FINDERS KEEPERS, MR...

I HAVE NO NAME, PRINCESS. NOT SINCE I WAS A CHILD.

CALL ME WHAT YOU WILL.

BUT OTHERS HAVE CALLED ME **STALKER.**

HE KNOWS WHO I *AM.*

WHAT IS IT YOU **WANT** FROM ME, SWORDBEARER?

YOUR LIFE, PROBABLY.

BUT IN FINE SERVICE, AND FOR MEANINGFUL REWARD.

I WANT YOU TO SAVE THIS WORLD.
AND STILL OTHERS, YET UNKNOWN TO YOU.

YOU DOUBT. OF COURSE YOU DOUBT.
USE THE CORD, PRINCESS. WRAP IT ABOUT ME AND KNOW THE TRUTH.

PEOPLE HAVE MADE THIS REQUEST BEFORE, TO THEIR REGRET.
THE LASSO TREATS THOSE WHO TRY TO DECEIVE IT WITH BRUTAL REGARD.

BUT IT IS ALWAYS MY INCLINATION TO BELIEVE.
DIANA! NO!

OH.
NO.
THE END OF THE EARTH IS BUT AN EDGE, PRINCESS.
YOU STAND AT ITS PRECIPICE, LOOKING DOWN.

DIANA.
OH, LORD, WE NEED A MEDIC.
OR AN EXORCIST.
THAT WAS NOT VERY WISE OF HER, I MUST SAY. PERHAPS SHE'S NOT THE ONE, AFTER ALL.

YOU JUST SHUT YOUR MOUTH, MISTER.
OR SWORD OR NOT, YOU'LL REGRET IT.
MM.
I DON'T THINK SHE'S BREATHING.

HE...
HE HASN'T GOT...

HE HAS NO SOUL.

LET GO OF HER. LET HER GO. WHATEVER YOU'RE DOING...
MM. I THINK NOT.
LOST, SHE IS. LOST SHE MAY REMAIN.

IF YOU'RE CONSIDERING REMOVING THE CORD... I WOULDN'T.
I THINK IT MIGHT DO HER SOME EVIL.

YOU GO STRAIGHT TO HELL, MISTER.
I'LL FIND HER.

UNTOLD AGES HE HAS LIVED.
WITH NO LOVE.
NO JOY.
'TIL HE'S FORGOTTEN THE VALUE OF SUCH THINGS.

NO BEING HAS SUFFERED SO, NOT IN HISTORY.
POOR, PITIFUL, WRETCHED PRESENCE!
IT IS TOO MUCH. INDESCRIBABLE.
ENDLESS.
ENDLESS.
DIANA. DIAANNNNAA!

I...
I FEEL IT. A WHISPER OF WHAT IT MEANS TO BE *HIM*.
LIKE MY HEART BLEEDS *OUT* ALL REASON TO *LIVE*.
THE HORIZON... THE *BLACK HORIZON*.
DIANA!

I'M *HERE*. I'M *HERE*.
THE ICE. THE DEEP FROST.
DO YOU FEEL IT, ETTA?

DIANA!
DO YOU FEEL THE BITTER COLD?

"I DON'T THINK I'LL EVER BE WARM AGAIN, ETTA."
FOR FIVE DAYS, I CHASED THE DEMON ON FOOT.

MOUNTAINS DID I CLIMB.
GREAT RIVERS DID I SWIM.

DRAGONS HAVE I FOUGHT.
MY OWN NEPHEW WAS ROASTED AND EATEN BEFORE I SLAYED THAT SERPENT.

WHAT DO YOU SAY OF MY SUFFERING, WENCH?
ME?
I'D SAY IT WENT A BIT WORSE FOR YOUR NEPHEW.
WELL.
YOU HAVE DONE A SIMPLE THING, BUT ONE THAT MANY HAVE REGRETTED, SLATTERN.

YOU HAVE MANAGED TO ANNOY ME.
I CAN ONLY.... HUHH.
HUMBLY APOLOGIZE, LORD.
I FEEL IT. IN MY HEART. THE COLD.
THE DESIRE TO KILL MY ENEMIES
STALKER'S "GIFT" TO ME.
THE BLACK HORIZON.
AARRRRRHH!

I DEEM YOU ILL-USED, GIRL.
I COULD FIND BUT MANY HAPPIER USES FOR YOU.
HE CAN'T KNOW. THERE IS NOTHING IN HIS EXPERIENCE THE LIKES OF WHAT I AM BECOMING, FROM STALKER'S TOUCH.
POWERS OR NOT. MISSION OR NOT. TRAINING OR NOT...
...THIS MAN HAS NEVER LOOKED AT HIS OWN DEATH IN SUCH PROXIMITY.
FIERCE LITTLE SCRATCHER, AREN'T YOU?
FUNNY, I WAS ABOUT TO SAY YOU MIGHT TRY BEING SOMETHING OTHER THAN A WARRIOR, YOURSELF.
BUT YOU'RE TOO UGLY TO BE A WHORE.
UHGH.
HEH.
HOLD, WARRIOR.
I ERRED.
I AM TIRED BEYOND MEASURE, BUT BEOWULF, I REMAIN.
I DO NOT FIGHT WOMEN.

I SEE, LORD.
DO YOU EVER, BY CHANCE, FIGHT BESIDE WOMEN?
THE PEASANTS, BEOWULF.
AYE?
THEY ARE WORSHIPPERS OF GRENDEL. I HEARD THEM TELL TALES OF HIS PRAISE AS I ENTERED THIS PLACE.
AYE.
I'M SORRY ABOUT YOUR NEPHEW.
TRUTH BE TOLD?
I NEVER REALLY LIKED HIM.
IT CALLS TO ME, THE TASTE FOR WAR.
OH, MOTHER. WHAT HAVE I DONE?

US NEWS
I GOT HER OUT. WHY ISN'T SHE MOVING?
WHAT'S WRONG WITH HER?

IT IS WHAT HAD TO HAPPEN. I HAD NO CHOICE.
HER COMPASSION MADE HER...
...UNABLE TO COMPLETE THE JOB AT HAND.

DIANA?
SWEETIE, WAKE UP.
The cold... I sseee the horizon, we're rushing towards it...

WHAT IS IT YOU WANT? WHAT IS IT YOU WANT HER TO DO?
THERE'S SOMETHING I NEED HER TO KILL.
ON MY WORLD, HE IS KNOWN AS D'GRTH.

I BELIEVE YOU CALL HIM THE DEVIL.

WONDER WOMAN #21 Cover by Aaron Lopresti with Alex Sinclair

DEPARTMENT OF METAHUMAN AFFAIRS.
TAKE A WALK WITH ME, SPECIAL AGENT TRESSER.
UNLESS YOU'RE IN THE MIDDLE OF MORE PRESSING MATTERS?
DIRECTOR STEEL.
UH, NO. WAIT. SURE. I MEAN...
YEAH.
WE HAVE A BIT OF A PROBLEM, TOM.
WE DO?
CENTRAL SAYS YOU'RE NOT TURNING IN YOUR FIELD PAPERWORK.
OH. RIGHT. ABOUT THAT...
I DIDN'T HIRE YOU FOR YOUR FILING SKILLS, AGENT TRESSER.
NO ONE DOES, REALLY.
EXACTLY.
I FEEL LIKE SHOOTING SOMETHING. DO YOU MIND?
NO, NO. BY ALL MEANS. FIRE AWAY.
FIRING RANGE
DO YOU LOVE YOUR COUNTRY, TOM?
I DON'T QUITE GET...
IT'S A SIMPLE QUESTION.

YES. YES, I LOVE MY COUNTRY.
AT EASE, SOLDIER.
I DIDN'T HIRE YOU FOR YOUR PATRIOTISM, EITHER. A FEW ROUNDS?
NO, I'M FINE. THANKS JUST THE SAME.
ALL RIGHT, THEN, LET ME JUST ASK...

WHAT *DID* YOU HIRE ME FOR?
A FAIR QUESTION.

I HIRED YOU BECAUSE YOU'RE THE BEST DAMN ESPIONAGE AGENT I'VE EVER SEEN. BEST I'VE EVER *HEARD* OF.
EVEN *WITHOUT* YOUR... "DISGUISES," YOU...
...WELL, YOU'RE SNEAKY AS ALL HELL, TRESSER.
SO I HAVE A QUESTION, AND A PROPOSITION, AND THEN WE FORGET THIS CONVERSATION EVER HAPPENED, AGREED?

LOOK ME IN THE EYES WHEN YOU ANSWER, PLEASE.
YEAH. OKAY.
AGREED.
THERE'S A CONSPIRACY, TOM.
OUR HIGHEST GOVERNMENTAL AGENCIES ARE BEING INFILTRATED.

THIS ISN'T CROP CIRCLES OR BOYS FROM BRAZIL, SON.
IT'S HAPPENING. WE'RE ALL AT RISK. I BELIEVE *TWO* SUCH SLEEPER AGENTS ARE IN OUR MIDST ALREADY.
I CAN'T HAVE THAT.

AGENTS DIANA PRINCE AND ETTA CANDY-TREVOR, IN POINT OF FACT.
WHAT? NO. DIRECTOR STEEL, ALL DUE RESPECT... I'M SUPPOSED TO BELIEVE PRINCE AND CANDY ARE, WHAT, COMMUNISTS?
NO, TOM. MUCH, MUCH WORSE.

I BELIEVE THEY'RE BOTH AMAZONS.

THINK OF IT, TOM. DO YOU KNOW THE TECHNOLOGY THEY HAVE?
ARE WE TO BELIEVE AN ISLAND NATION THAT EXPORTS NOTHING BUT WAR AND FAIRY PRINCESSES, A NATION THAT RECENTLY ATTACKED OUR CAPITAL AND THEN COMPLETELY DISAPPEARED, IS SUDDENLY BACK IN THE PEACE-AND-LOVE BUSINESS?

I NEED THEM SURVEILLED. I NEED EVIDENCE, AND RIGHT DAMN QUICK, BEFORE WE GET AMAZONS ATTACK, THE SEQUEL.
I NEED A BASTARD, TOM. I NEED SOMEONE WHO WOULD GIVE UP HIS OWN MOTHER TO SERVE THE MISSION.
CONGRATULATIONS. THAT BASTARD IS YOU.

SAY I BELIEVE YOU, DIRECTOR.
WHAT ABOUT PROCEDURE? WHAT ABOUT DUE PROCESS? HOW TOXIC AM I ALLOWED TO GO?
WHY NOT FIRE A COUPLE ROUNDS? IT MIGHT MAKE YOU LESS TENSE.
THE SAFETY'S OFF ON YOUR WEAPON, SPECIAL AGENT. COMPLETELY OFF.

IT MIGHT MAKE A LOT OF PEOPLE LESS TENSE.
GET A COUPLE GOOD MEN. THAT'S MEN, TOM.
START WITH PRINCE.
SHE KNEW FAR TOO MUCH ABOUT GORILLA GRODD'S OPERATIONS AND COULDN'T EXPLAIN WHY. THEY MAY BE WORKING TOGETHER. KEEP AN EYE ON HER.

"I WANT TO KNOW WHERE SHE IS AT ALL TIMES."
I'VE LOST MY STRENGTH HERE, ON THIS PLANE.
AND THAT'S NOT ALL I'VE LOST.
KILL! KILL! DRINK THEIR FILTHY BLOOD!
SLASH THEM BOTH!
PROTECT OUR LORD! SAVE THE LINE OF CAIN!
MY COMPASSION. MY MERCY. MY LOVE.
I CAN FEEL THEM SLOWLY SLIPPING AWAY FROM ME LIKE SAND THROUGH MY OPENED FINGERS.
AND THAT MIGHT BE THE WOUND THAT FINALLY SLAYS WHAT I TRULY AM.
ENDS OF THE EARTH
PART 2 of 4
THE EDGE OF INSANITY

OR EVEN WORSE STILL...
IT IS NO MORE THAN YOU DESERVE, DOG!
ARRAHH!
...THAT PART MAY ALREADY BE DEAD.

THE BLACK HORIZON.
I DO NOT YET KNOW WHAT IT MEANS.
BUT ITS HOLD ON MY SOUL IS UNRELENTING.
POX-CURSED TROLLOP!

I ASK YOU, DO ALL THE--
UHN--
--PROFESSIONAL SOLDIERS OF THIS TIME...

...ANNOUNCE THEIR AMBUSHES?
SEEMS A BIT OF A TACTICAL ERROR.
KRRAACK

YOU FIGHT WELL. I GIVE YOU MY RESPECT.
BUT WE HAVE ANOTHER PROBLEM.
ANOTHER, LORD BEOWULF? BEYOND BEING OUTNUMBERED TWENTY TO ONE?
I FEAR IT IS SO, FAIR ONE.

SORCERY!

IF ONE DELIBERATELY CHOOSES TO FIGHT A DEMON-WORSHIPPING CULT ALONGSIDE A LEGENDARY BARBARIAN WARRIOR LORD...
YES. SORCERY.
...ONE CAN HARDLY COMPLAIN WHEN THE RESULTS ARE UNORTHODOX.

I WAS GOING TO SAY, PERHAPS AN HONORABLE RETREAT MIGHT BE IN ORDER.
RETREAT? WHEN THERE'S DEMON BLOOD TO SPILL?
AAAUCKK!

WELL. IT CAN'T BE HELPED.

I'VE HAD SOME SMALL DEALINGS WITH IT IN THE PAST.
NEVERTHELESS.
MIGHT I SUGGEST PERHAPS--

UNN.
I FORGET. FORGET WHAT IT'S LIKE TO HAVE TO *DODGE.*
MEAT AND BONE, MEAT AND BONE, WENCH!
DO YOU NOT KNOW, DEMON?
DO YOU NOT *KNOW* WHOM YOU *FACE?*

TELL THEM IN THE AFTERLIFE, SERPENT.
TELL THEM DIANA, PRINCESS OF THEMYSCIRA SENT YOU TO YOUR GOD-CURSED END!

JUST AS ALL WOMEN.
HE CUT ME. HE MUST... HE HAS TO PAY.
YOU TALK WHEN YOU SHOULD ACT.
MY ALLY NOW BETRAYS ME?
YES, WELL. KILL HIM AFTER WE FIND EGRESS.
THE MEAD HALL BURNS AND I HAVE NO WISH TO REMAIN AS WITNESS.
HE... HE SEEKS ONLY TO AID ME. TO SAVE ME.
HOW COULD I HAVE SEEN THIS AS A THREAT?
I AM NO LONGER MYSELF.
LOOSE THEIR HORSES.
WE'LL MAKE FOR THE MOUNTAINS!
HOW DID I LET THIS HAPPEN?

WAIT.

HOLD, LORD BEOWULF.

THEY'RE NOT FOLLOWING.

I...
...I WANT TO THANK YOU. FOR WHAT YOU DID BACK THERE.
'TIS NOTHING, I MERELY FOUND THE QUICKEST WAY *OUT*.
AYE.
NO DOUBT THEY LEAVE OUR TENDER FATE TO THEIR *MASTER*.

NO, SIRE. I MEAN THAT MAN, THAT BEING.
I WOULD HAVE KILLED HIM, BUT FOR YOU.
HUR.
A FAT HOG FART'S WORTH OF SHAME *THAT* WOULD HAVE BEEN, EH?
I'D HAVE GUTTED HIM *MYSELF* WERE OUR ACCOMMODATIONS A BIT LESS SHARP AND SCORCHED.
WHAT *EXACTLY* IS IT YOU'RE DOING, FAIR ONE?
CALL ME DIANA, PLEASE, LORD.
AND I DO WHAT I ALWAYS DO WHEN I FIND MYSELF LOST.
I'M ATTEMPTING TO PRAY.
KANE MILOHAI, FATHER OF THE EARTH AND HEAVENS, PLEASE HEAR YOUR SERVANT. I AM WITHOUT A COMPASS AND CANNOT SEE THE SUN. I ASK OF THEE THE ALLOWANCE TO COMPLETE MY TASK, BEFORE THE SOUL THAT I AM IS GONE.
I'VE NOT HEARD OF THIS GOD.
YOU WOULDN'T HAVE. I'VE ONLY RECENTLY MET HIM MYSELF.
HE GAVE ME THE STANDARD I WEAR ON MY ARM.
I CONFESS THAT I HAVE NEVER TRUSTED RELIGIOUS CONVERTS.
ABANDONED YOU, YOUR PREVIOUS MASTERS?
THEY... THEY DO NOT ANSWER MY CALLS. MY MOTHER WAS IN DESPERATE NEED. I HAD NO CHOICE.
HUR.
SO WE ARE FICKLE, THEN, TOO?

CURSE ME FOR UNDERESTIMATING THIS MAN, THIS LEADER OF MEN.
NO MERE BARBARIAN IS HE. HE SEES MUCH AND CUTS DEEPLY, WITH BLADE OR TONGUE.
BEWARE, DIANA.
I HAVE MADE MY CHOICE. IF THERE ARE CONSEQUENCES, I ALONE SHALL BEAR THEM.
AH, BUT THAT IS ALMOST NEVER THE CASE, THAT LAST.
"DIANA."

THERE IS SOME DEBATE ABOUT YOU, LORD.
ABOUT WHETHER YOU ARE CHRISTIAN OR PAGAN.
IS THERE?
HOW INTERESTING.
AND YET HE GIVES AWAY NOTHING. THERE ARE LESSONS TO BE LEARNED HERE.

I KNOW YOU HIDE SECRETS, WOMAN.
I HAVE ENEMIES. AND THEY WOULD NOT BE ABOVE SENDING A BEAUTIFUL COURTESAN TO STAB ME IN MY SLEEP.
A WOMAN WHO ABANDONS HER GODS MIGHT SIMILARLY BE FAITHLESS TO HER COMPANIONS.

I WARN YOU, SIRE.
I HAVE TRIED TO BE RESPECTFUL.

BUT I WILL NOT BE HANDLED.
THE BLOOD. I CAN ALMOST SMELL IT.
BUT THEN I SEE WHAT I HAD BEEN PRAYING FOR.

MY CONSTELLATION.
THE W.
THE CROWN.
CASSIOPEIA.
IT'S DIFFERENT HERE, SLIGHTLY OUT OF ALIGNMENT.
BUT IT'S THERE, THE CONSTELLATION OF MY BIRTH.

BLESS AND KEEP YOU, KANE MILOHAI, KINDEST OF ALL GODS. I HEAR YOUR MESSAGE AND ACCEPT YOUR COMFORT.
STAY YOUR BLADE, SIRE.

THE TRUTH IS, I'VE COME TO ASK YOUR AID.
WELL, THAT'S NOT ENTIRELY TRUE, IS IT?

WE'VE COME TO BEG, HAVEN'T WE?
FOR THE LIVES OF ALL THE PEOPLE OF ALL THE KNOWN WORLDS.
IT IS THE MAN WITH NO NAME. THE STALKER.
HE WHO BROUGHT ME HERE, AND WHOSE BLACK EMPTINESS HAS INFECTED MY OWN SPIRIT.

I'VE TRAVELED...FARTHER AND LONGER THAN YOU MAY IMAGINE, POET LORD.
WILL YOU HEAR MY TALE?
THEN AFTER, BY ALL MEANS, SLAY US BOTH IF YOU MUST.
I REALLY MUST REMEMBER.
IN THE FUTURE, HE MUST LET ME DO THE TALKING.

WASHINGTON, D.C.
"KEEP AN EYE ON HER, TOM. SHE'S DANGEROUS, TOM. A THREAT TO NATIONAL SECURITY, TOM."
A THREAT TO INSOMNIA IS WHAT SHE IS.

"PLEASE BITE ME, DIRECTOR," I SHOULD HAVE SAID. "I HATE STAKEOUTS, DIRECTOR," I COULD HAVE ADDED.
"THIS MISSION IS A DANGER TO MY FAT BEHIND, DIRECTOR," I COULD HAVE OFFERED HELPFULLY.
"AND SHE DOES HAPPEN TO BE MY PARTNER, DIRECTOR," I COULD HAVE POINTED OUT.

HANG ON.

LOLLY LOLLY LOLLY GET YOUR STRANGE BEDFELLOWS HERE.

EST. HEIGHT 7' 4"... EST. WEIGHT 820 LBS 6 OZ
HOLY CRAP.

THIS IS NEMESIS REQUESTING DIRECTOR STEEL IMMEDIATELY.
TELL HIM THE SIGHTING IS CONFIRMED.
DIRECTOR STEEL IS UNAVAILABLE, AGENT TRESSER. DO YOU REQUIRE BACKUP?
HELL YES, SEND EVERYONE. IT'S GRODD, COPY?
GORILLA GRODD!

I DON'T BELIEVE FOR A SECOND YOU'RE ALIGNED WITH A MONSTER LIKE GRODD, PRINCE.
NOT WILLINGLY.

SO THAT MEANS BLACKMAIL. OR KIDNAPPING. OR WORSE.
AND I'M NOT LETTING YOU BE TORTURED BY THAT ANIMAL WHILE I WAIT AROUND DAINTILY FOR BACKUP.

FREEZE, YOU *&?&?% FUZZBALL!

UH.
NOT THAT A *&?&?% FUZZBALL IS A BAD THING, EXACTLY...

I COME FROM... SOMEPLACE ELSE. AND SOME OTHER *WHEN*, AS WELL.
AS A CHILD, I MADE A POOR BARGAIN WITH A DEMON. I WAS HUNGRY, AND HAD NO WISDOM.
I GAINED SKILLS, BUT AT THE EXPENSE OF MY IMMORTAL SOUL.
"I WAS BETRAYED, AS SELFISH FOOLS HAVE ALWAYS BEEN BETRAYED.
"I SEARCHED THE ENDS OF MY WORLD IN A VAIN ATTEMPT TO REGAIN WHAT I HAD LOST, AND ENDED AT *GERANTH*, IN THE COLD WASTES.
"THE CITY OF *TEMPLES* IS THAT HARD PLACE.
"THERE, IN THE POOREST OF ALL SITES OF WORSHIP, TO THE HUMBLEST AND MOST CRINGING OF GODLINGS, THERE WAS YET A *SEER*.
"AN *ORACLE*, IF YOU WILL.
"WHO HELD AN INHUMAN QUANTITY OF KNOWLEDGE, IT WAS SAID."
SEER. I COME TO...
I KNOW WHAT YOU SEEK, WARRIOR.
AND I KNOW WHAT YOU FEAR.
THEN YOU KNOW *NOTHING*, WENCH, AS I *FEAR* NOTHING.
REALLY?
NOT EVEN...

...THE DEVIL WHO LEASHED YOUR SOUL, STALKER?
THE HOURGLASS OF REALITY DRAINS, WARRIOR.
DGRTH WILL CLAIM ALL WORLDS AND ALL DIMENSIONS AS HIS OWN.
HE TIRES OF WAITING. HE WANTS TO DEVOUR ALL.
MY LIFE IS NOTHING. I WANT ONLY WHAT HE TOOK FROM ME.
IS THERE NO WAY TO STOP HIM?
THERE IS A WAY. HE CAN ONLY BE KILLED ON THE STONE ALTAR AT THE END OF THE WORLD.
YOU WILL NEED THREE OTHER... PARTICULAR SWORDBEARERS.

FOOLISH *WENCH.*
WHY SHOULD I TRUST ONE SUCH AS *YOU?*

WHY, OH, YOU CREATURE OF VIOLENCE, YOU THOUGHTLESS AND USELESS AVATAR OF THE BUZZARD'S GLUTTONY OF BATTLEFIELD *GLORY?*

WHY MIGHT A GIFTED, BUT SIMPLE *ORACLE* SUCH AS MYSELF WANT THE GREAT BEAST *DEAD?*

BECAUSE I *TOO* WAS A GREEDY *FOOL.*
IT'S NOT JUST *MEN* WHO MAKE POOR *BARGAINS* WITH DEMONS, WARRIOR.

IT WAS THE *ORACLE* WHO ADAPTED YOUR GARB AND SPEECH FOR THIS JOURNEY, DIANA.

SHE WAS QUITE MAD.
BUT EVERYTHING SHE FORETOLD HAS COME TO PASS.
SHE SAID *YOU* WOULD PAY AN *ESPECIALLY* DEAR PRICE, PRINCESS.

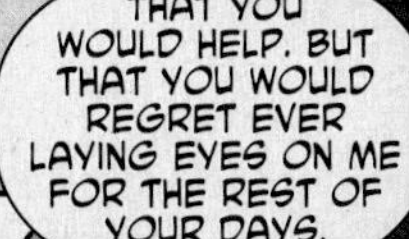
THAT YOU WOULD HELP. BUT THAT YOU WOULD REGRET EVER LAYING EYES ON ME FOR THE REST OF YOUR DAYS.

I DON'T NEED THE LASSO TO KNOW THAT BEOWULF WILL AGREE.
HE REGARDS HIS WILL TO HELP THE DEFENSELESS AS A BURDEN HE CAN'T AVOID.
I MIGHT CALL IT BY A DIFFERENT NAME.
NOBILITY.
IF THIS... "DGRTH" HUNGERS FOR THE END OF TIMES, PERHAPS WE SHOULD HAVE A POLITE DISCUSSION WITH HIM. PERHAPS NOT. PERHAPS IT IS ALL TROUGH-SPITTLE.
FOR ARGUMENT'S SAKE, HOW EXACTLY MIGHT WE TRAVEL TO THIS OTHER PLANE?
SHE GAVE ME THIS.
NO MORE PRECIOUS STONE EXISTS ANYWHERE IN THIS OR ANOTHER UNIVERSE.
IT IS THE SOUL OF THE ROCK OF ETERNITY. THERE IS ONE IN EVERY DIMENSION, EVERY PLANE OF EXISTENCE.
IT IS THE STONE HEART OF THE AGES. WITH DIANA'S SHELL VEHICLE, IT WILL GUIDE US ANYWHERE.
WILL YOU HELP US, LORD? FOR THE SAKE OF YOUR PEOPLE, AND ALL SUCH PEOPLE YET TO BE?
...
I'M GOING TO MISS THIS MOUNT. A NOBLE BEAST.
AND WHERE IS THIS CONTRIVANCE, THIS "VEHICLE," THAT OUR FINE LADY SEEMS TO CARRY ABOUT HER PERSON?
FUNNY YOU SHOULD ASK THAT QUESTION, ACTUALLY.
OUR JOURNEY IS LONG...

AND WITH A SPEED I'D NOT THOUGHT POSSIBLE...
COWARDLY DOGS! ATTACKERS FROM THE SHADOW!
I'LL SLAY YOU ALL!
...I'VE AGAIN SOMEHOW MANAGED TO OFFEND.
AND THIS ONE MIGHT BE THE EQUAL OF US ALL.
SORCEROUS WENCH!
WE PREFER TO BE...UGH!
...PREFER TO BE CALLED TROLLOPS.

IF YOU DON'T MIND.
THE LASSO. I CAN BIND HIM. MAKE HIM SEE REASON.

WELL SAID, SIRE.
WHAT?
THE LASSO. HEPHAESTUS' GIFT.

IT...
IT'S REJECTING ME!
DIANA.
PERHAPS, THE BATTLE, ONCE AGAIN?
YES. THE BATTLE.

I HAD *FORGOTTEN* FOR A MOMENT.

TELL ME, DIANA. THE WOMEN WHERE YOU ARE FROM, ARE THEY ALL...
I HAVE MANY HUNDREDS OF SISTERS, LORD.
HUR.
I DO NOT THINK I WOULD LIKE IT MUCH THERE.
THE *DEFORMITY.* IT IS *HE* WHOM WE *SEEK.*

MAY I SUGGEST WE LIFT THE BRUTE'S HEAD OUT OF THE WATER AND PROCEED TO THE STONE ALTAR AND *FINISH* THIS THING ONCE AND FOR...
...
WHAT *IS* IT?
YOUR... YOUR *HAND,* DIANA.
IN *WYRD'S* NAME, LOOK AT YOUR *HAND!*

OH, MOTHER. MY QUEEN.
WHAT IS IT THAT I AM BECOMING?

THEMYSCIRA.
MY DAUGHTER HAS NOT RETURNED.
YOUR WISH CAME TRUE, AT LEAST TEMPORARILY, ALKYONE. SHE LIVES, BUT HAS CHOSEN THE OUTSIDE WORLD. AGAIN
WE ARE ALONE, IF YOU YET LIVE.
I DO NOT BELIEVE THE MEGALODONS DEVOURED YOU, QUEENSGUARD.
MY CAPTAIN. MY PROTECTOR.
EH?
IT'S THE CROWN SHE MADE ME, CARVED WITH HER OWN TEETH.
BUT I DESTROYED THIS... I CRACKED IT IN TWO.
I COMMAND THEE... SHOW YOURSELF.

OH.
ATHENA FORGIVE ME.
SHE LIVES. SHE LIVES.

WONDER WOMAN #22 Cover by Aaron Lopresti

A QUEEN I MIGHT BE.

ALL-POWERFUL AND UNQUESTIONED, FOR AN ETERNITY AND MORE BESIDES.

IF I CHOOSE TO STAY IN THIS REALM AND DIMENSION.

WITH MY ENEMIES IN THE ACCOMMODATIONS THEY MOST DESERVE.

AND A MYRIAD OF SUITORS AWAITING MY AMUSEMENT.

IF I WERE TO STAY. IF I WERE TO POSSESS THE BIT OF THE ROCK OF ETERNITY THAT HANGS ON A THREAD AROUND THE STALKER'S THROAT.
SO SIMPLE A THING, TO SLIT THAT THROAT AND TAKE IT.
MOTHER.
YOUR RADIANT MAJESTY.
AND THAT'S THE THING, THE PAINFUL REALIZATION.

I FEAR THAT MY WORLD, MY FORMER HOME...?
IT MAY NO LONGER HAVE A PLACE FOR ME.
IT IS A GOOD DAY, MOTHER.
I DECLARE IT A CELEBRATION.
BRING THE PEOPLE HERE THAT THEY MAY SHOW THEIR LOVE AND FEALTY.
ENDS OF THE EARTH
PART 3 of 4

AS YOU WISH, YOUR RADIANT MAJESTY.

THE REBELS HAVE BEEN BROUGHT TO HEEL, YOUR RADIANT MAJESTY. YOUR NAVY HAS CAPTURED MANY SCORE OF PRISONERS.
WE ARE NOT WITHOUT MERCY, ARTEMIS.
THEY WILL BE *TAUGHT* TO LOVE ME, THOSE THAT SURVIVE.

YOUR RADIA...
DAUGHTER.
PERMISSION TO SPEAK.
IT IS GRANTED.

DAUGHTER!

WHY DO YOU WEEP, MOTHER?
THIS WORLD KNOWS PEACE NOW. AND THROUGH DISCIPLINE, WILL LEARN THE AMAZON WAY.
WHY DO YOU WEEP?

I FEAR YOU WILL LOSE YOURSELF AND EVERYTHING THAT IS DIANA.
I HAVE LIVED MANY LIVES, DAUGHTER. I HAVE EXPERIENCED THINGS YOU HAVE NOT YET SEEN.
AND I WARN YOU, THROUGH VEIL OF DREAM AND TIME...

DO NOT TRUST THE RED-EYED MAN!

SHE'S RIGHT, YOU KNOW.

YOU DON'T REALLY KNOW A THING ABOUT ME.
YOUR *MAJESTY*.
THIS IS THE MAN.
THE REASON I'M OUT OF MY TIME AND PLACE.
THE REASON I AM LOSING MYSELF.

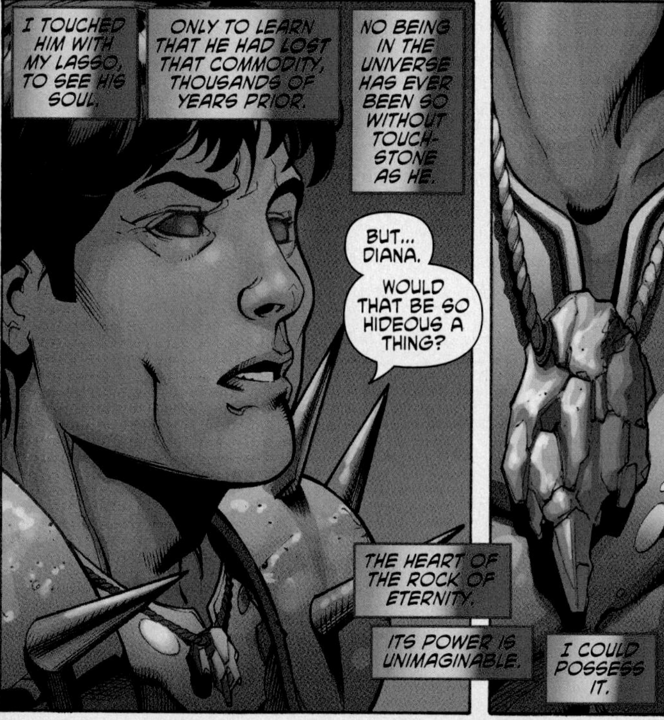
I TOUCHED HIM WITH MY LASSO, TO SEE HIS SOUL.
ONLY TO LEARN THAT HE HAD LOST THAT COMMODITY, THOUSANDS OF YEARS PRIOR.
NO BEING IN THE UNIVERSE HAS EVER BEEN SO WITHOUT TOUCHSTONE AS HE.
BUT... DIANA.
WOULD THAT BE SO HIDEOUS A THING?
THE HEART OF THE ROCK OF ETERNITY.
ITS POWER IS UNIMAGINABLE.
I COULD POSSESS IT.

HIS SOULLESSNESS HAS INFECTED ME, SO THAT I AM LOSING RECOGNITION OF EVERYTHING FAMILIAR TO MY HEART.
SO THAT I AM FINDING THAT COMPASSION TASTES LIKE ASH ON MY TONGUE.
EVEN LOVE.
TO HAVE EVERYTHING YOU WANT...TO TEACH YOUR LESSONS EVEN TO THOSE TOO STUBBORN TO HEAR?
TO RIGHT ANCIENT WRONGS, AND FREE CAPTIVES OF ANTIQUITY?

TO STAY AND TO LEAD... BY MY SIDE?
I CANNOT LOVE YOU, PRINCESS. THAT PART OF ME WAS GIVEN TO THE DEMON D'GRTH AGES HENCE.
BUT I PROMISE I WILL NEVER *LEAVE* YOU.

MY MOTHER. MY SISTERS. CASSIE. DONNA. TOM. ETTA.

I AM FORGETTING WHAT THOSE WORDS *MEAN*.

THIS IS HOW IT BEGINS.

THE WAKING DREAMS. I KNOW. I KNOW.

CHERISH EVEN YOUR NIGHTMARES, PRINCESS. YOU WILL SOON NOT EVEN HAVE *THEM* FOR COMPANIONSHIP.

TAKE SOME WINE. I'M TOLD IT HELPS.

WHERE... WHERE ARE THE OTHERS, STALKER?

I WAS RAISED BY NO ONE, PRINCESS, AND GIVEN NO NAME.
I LIVED IN POVERTY NEITHER OF YOUR CULTURE CAN IMAGINE.
I SUFFERE
EVEN BEFORE I LOST MY SOUL, I'M NOT CERTAIN I EVEN EXISTED, SO EMPTY WAS MY IDENTITY.
THAT IS WHAT YOU TOUCHED, WHEN YOU PUT THIS WEAPON ON ME.
THAT IS WHAT YOU CONSUMED, MADE A PART OF YOU.
YOUR LASSO ISN'T ANGRY, PRINCESS.
IT SIMPLY CANNOT *FIND* YOU IN THE DARK.
AH. THE TRICKSTER WENCH APPROACHES.
YOU'LL NOT CATCH ME UNAWARES AGAIN, TROLLOP.
ODD HOW LIMITED MEN'S VOCABULARIES BECOME WHEN FACED WITH A WOMAN WHO IS THEIR BETTER.
OF COURSE, IF YOU'D LIKE ME TO KNOCK YOU SENSELESS AGAIN?
HROTHGAR'S OATH. KNOW YOU NOT A MATTER OF *IMPORT* FROM A MATTER OF *INCONSEQUENCE?*
YOU'RE WORSE THAN A DRUNKEN GARRISON OF SPEAR-DANES, *EACH* OF YOU.
THINK YOU OF *HONOR* AND *GLORY,* IF *DUTY* IS BEYOND YOUR KEN.
WE PRESS *ON,* TO SEE THIS... *"ORACLE."*
I AM NOT YOUR ENEMY, CLAW. I SAY IN FACT THAT THIS DEMON'S CURSE BINDS US *TOGETHER,* SOMEHOW.
I HAVE BEEN DECEIVED BEFORE, WOMAN.
BETRAY ME AT YOUR PERIL.

ICHAR, THE THRONE-CITY OF PYTHARIA, LIES JUST WEST OF THESE DUNES. THAT'S WHERE THE WITCH YOU SEEK PLIES HER TRADE.
STALKER, I THOUGHT YOU SAID THAT THIS "ORACLE" WAS FROM *YOUR* WORLD?
AS FAR AS I HAVE SEEN, SHE REMAINS A CONSTANT. A PRESENCE LIKE HER EXISTS ON EVERY PLANE.
EVEN YOURS, I SUSPECT.
AH.
AND SO I FOLLOW. AND SO I TRUST.

WHAT *CHOICE* DO I *HAVE?*
I PLACE FAITH IN NEITHER OF THEM.
AYE. YET... IF TRUTHFUL THEY *ARE*, THEN AID THEM WE *MUST*, OR THE COST IS EVERYTHING WE *KNOW*.
BY THE WAY, STALKER.
"ELPIS."
WHAT?

EVEN HERE, A PRINCESS I REMAIN. AND IT IS MY RIGHT TO GRANT NAMES AND HONORARIUMS AS I SEE FIT.
YOU SAID YOU HAD NEVER HAD A NAME. SO I GIVE YOU ONE FOR ALL TIME AND PURPOSE.
YOU ARE ELPIS, WHICH IN MY TONGUE MEANS, "HOPE."

WAIT. YOU CAN'T JUST... BUT I CAN'T...
I'VE HAD NO NAME FOR *EONS*. YOU THINK YOU CAN WAVE YOUR HAND AND *UNMAKE* ALL THAT, THAT *TIME*, THAT *MISERY*...
YOU CAN'T JUST...

"ELPIS."

DIANA PRINCE'S BROWNSTONE, WASHINGTON, D.C.
I could run.
I'm GOOD at running. And the dark?
I'm GOOD in the dark.
There's just one problem with that. Prince could be a hostage here, or WORSE.
No WAY I believe Steel's theory that she's on the BAD guys' side. And no WAY do I leave her in TROUBLE.
And that means...
...aw, hell. That means I play Tarzan with five superintel-ligent GORILLAS.
OKAY. ALL RIGHT, LET'S KEEP CALM.
THIS IS A LEXCORP MODEL D4 PROTOTYPE WITH ARMOR-PIERCING CONCUSSIVE BURST ENERGY SHELLS.
I'M GOING TO ASK ONE TIME.
WHERE IS AGENT PRINCE?
HE IS THE ONE HER MAJESTY DESIRES.
BUT HE IS WORKING AGAINST HER HERE, AND THIS IS HER NEST. HER DEN. WE MUST PROTECT IT!
HE IS FULL OF FEAR. AND HE IS NOT TO BE UNDERESTIMATED.
HE IS A HUMAN AND BARELY ABOVE THE RANK OF SUPPER!
WARMONGERING SUCCULENT!
I WARNED YOU.
AAAAAAAAAAAAAHHHH
Oh, man.
The smell of burnt FUR.

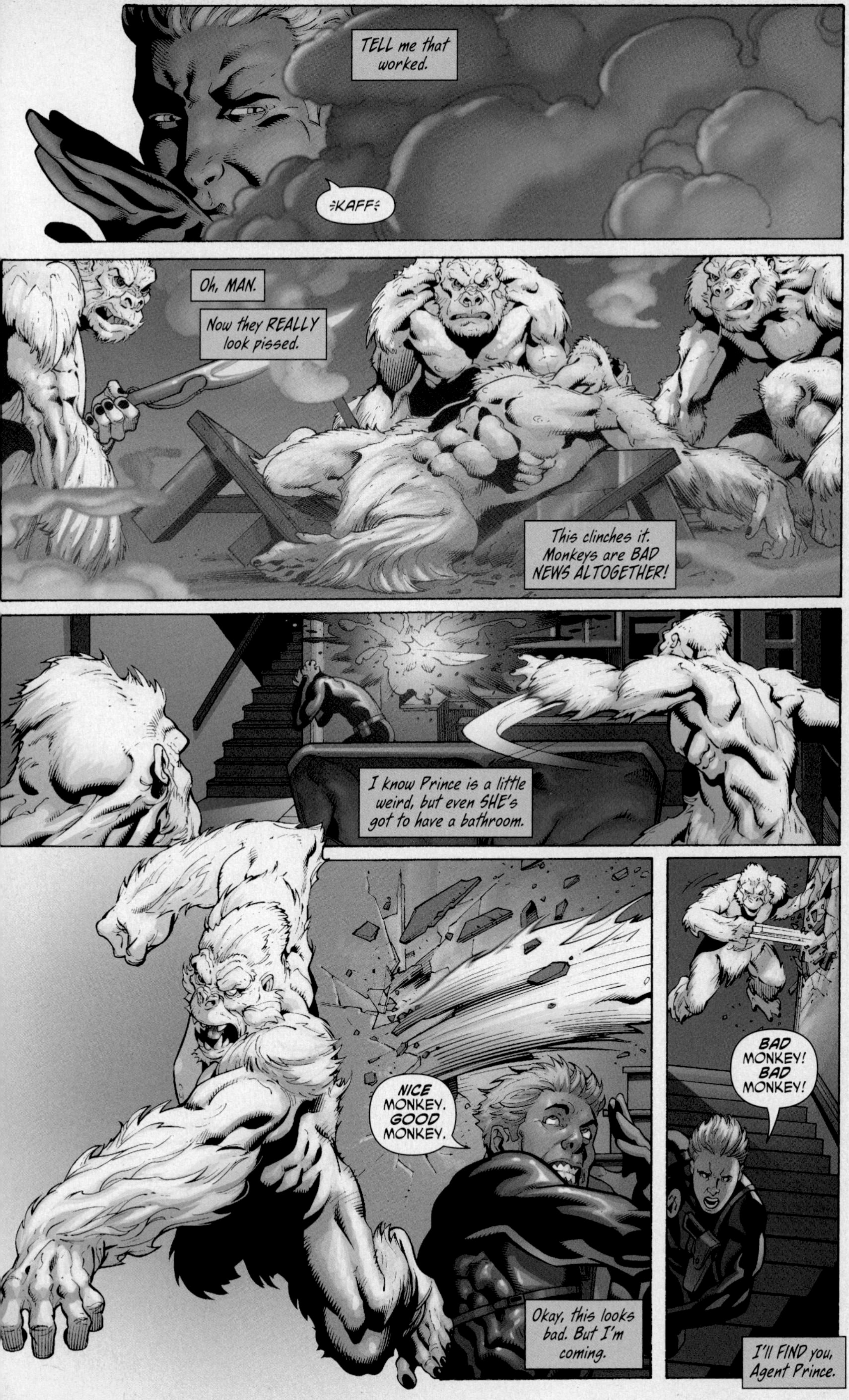

I know Prince is a little weird, but even SHE's got to have a bathroom.

NICE MONKEY. GOOD MONKEY.

Okay, this looks bad. But I'm coming.

BAD MONKEY! BAD MONKEY!

I'll FIND you, Agent Prince.

WHEREVER you are.

...ALL THE GOLD YOU CAN *STOMACH*, SEER, BUT FIRST, YOU TELL US WHAT WE NEED TO *KNOW.*

OH, I KNOW MUCH.

YES.

I KNOW YOU ALL DIE ALONE IN PAUPER'S GRAVES.

I KNOW THE GODS SEARCH FOR THAT ONE, IN A FLYING SHIP OF GOLD AND GREEN.
TAKE HER AWAY, THEY WILL, IF THEY SHOULD FIND HER.

AND I KNOW ONE FINAL SNIPPET, PETS.
I KNOW THAT D'GRTH KNOWS WHAT YOU PLAN.
HE WAITS FOR THEE AT THE STONE TABLE, ON A WORLD YOU HAVE YET TO ENCOUNTER...

WILL YOU GO TO FACE HIM, M
BRAVE, DOOME
COMPANY?

OPEN THE DOOR, HUMAN!

IN A MINUTE...!
THIS IS AGENT TRESSER AGAIN, REQUESTING A FULL RED ALERT AT THE HOME OF SPECIAL AGENT DIANA PRINCE.
PUT SOME FIRE UNDER THAT REQUEST, PLEASE!
PERFECT. Of COURSE, Prince is the only woman in D.C. without a MAKE-UP drawer!

Wait. Got it.
And she hasn't even OPENED it yet...?
PRINCE, I DON'T GET YA, BUT I LOVE YA.

WHAT? BUT... HOW...?
UM. OCCUPIED.
GRRRRR.
WHATEVER.
GRRR, AND ALL, I MEAN.

SNIFF
SNORT
WE ARE DECEIVED!
That's it, big boy. Keep SNIFFING.

MARI
Parfum
For She

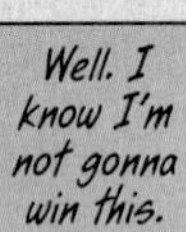
Well. I know I'm not gonna win this.

But maybe I can distract them long enough for the DMA to rescue PRINCE.
ARRGHHHHHH!
STINGS? YOU SHOULD TRY THE STYGIAN KILLER...

NEVER MIND.

HEADS UP, GUYS.

BOOM

ALL RIGHT, FLEABAGS... I GOT A LOT MORE WHERE THOSE CAME... FR...
... UMM...
EXCUSE ME, BUT IF IT'S NOT TOO MUCH TROUBLE--
--COULD SOMEONE PLEASE TELL ME WHAT THE HELL IS GOING ON HERE?

THIS... THIS IS IT. MY PREMONITION.

THE BLACK HORIZON.

YES.

OUR ROAD ENDS HERE, PRINCESS.

STALKER'S WORLD REMINDS ME OF APOKOLIPS, HOPELESS AND FORLORN AND LACKING ANYTHING THAT RESEMBLES BEAUTY.

UNN.
DIANA?

CLAW, ON THE OTHER HAND, SEEMS TO FIT THE ROLE OF HERO VERY POORLY INDEED.
IF SHE CANNOT WALK, THEN SHE CANNOT FIGHT.
WE'RE LIKELY DOING HER A KINDESS.
BUT IF IT'S THE STALKER WHO IS THE TRAITOR--HE WHO HOLDS THE SHARD THAT CONTROLS FORM AND TIME...
THE ORACLE SAID WE WERE ALL NEEDED.
ILL OR SOUND, SHE GOES.

I PITY HIM, THAT HE GREW UP HERE.

THE ORACLE SAID WE'D BE BETRAYED... BUT I LACK THE CONNECTION WITH MY LASSO TO KNOW WHO IS THE BETRAYER.

I CAN'T BELIEVE THAT BEOWULF WOULD DO SUCH A HING. HIS HEART IS TOO TRUE, HIS DESTINY TOO GREAT.
HOLD A MOMENT, BARBARIAN. SHE IS WITH FEVER.
LEAVE HER, THEN. LET HER STAY BEHIND.

...BUT THEN AN EVEN DARKER THOUGHT OCCURS TO ME.
THE DEMON'S CLAW CRAVES BLOOD AND POWER AT ALL TIMES, AND THE SHADOW ON MY SOUL HAS EATEN MY CONSCIENCE.
WHAT IF...
WHAT IF I AM THE BETRAYER?
I AM AN AMAZON.
WE DO NOT "STAY BEHIND."

MY WORLD IS UNLIKE YOURS, MY COMPANIONS. IT IS FLAT, LIKE A PARCHMENT, RATHER THAN SPHERICAL.
YOU SEE BEFORE YOU THE LITERAL END OF OUR EXISTENCE.
THAT'S IMPOSSIBLE, STALKER. THERE'S NO LOGIC IN THAT NOTION.
NEVERTHELESS, IT IS WHAT IT IS.
YOU TREAT YOUR ALLIES LITTLE BETTER THAN YOUR ENEMIES, SAVAGE ONE.
HMPH. I AGREED TO STOP THE SLAUGHTER OF ALL OUR WORLDS, YOUR "LORDSHIP."
IF I'D BEEN TOLD IN ADVANCE THAT *POLITENESS* WERE REQUIRED, I MIGHT WELL HAVE *REFUSED.*
EH EH EH EH. FOUR LOATHSOME TORTOISES, GOING NOWHERE, SEEING LITTLE AND HOPING NOTHING!
I BID YOU WELCOME, ALL OF YOU LOSSST SOULSSS.
YOU HAVE FOUND THE GRAVE WHERE YOU BELONG.
KINSLAYER! BLOODHUNGRY DEMON!
I'LL *GUT* YOU, GRENDEL, MISBEGOTTEN WHORESON OF *CAIN!*
AT LAST.
MY LITTLE SCATTERED TOY SOLDIERS, COME TO KILL THEIR MASTER.

COME, CHILDREN.
COME DRINK OF THE DEATH OF YOUR COMPANY!
FLESSHY MEWLING THINGSS, I GIVE YOU...
...THE HEART OF EVIL, MY DEMON LORD D'GRTH!
AHHK.
BEOWULF!

STALKER. THIS IS OUR TIME.
FIGHT WITH US!
FIGHT WITH YOU?

VERY WELL.
TRAITOROUS DOG!

GLCK.
TRAITOR! LIAR!

ALL THOSE AND MORE, LADY. WHEN I FOUND I COULD NOT DEFEAT THE DEVIL THAT STOLE MY SOUL, AFTER CENTURIES...
...I MADE A BARGAIN. YOU, THE PROPHESIED WARRIORS WHO COULD KILL HIM, AND THE ETERNITY SHARD, FOR THE COST OF ONE SMALL SOUL.
YOU, WHO HAVE ONLY TASTED MY EMPTY EXISTENCE, CAN NEVER KNOW WHAT THE CENTURIES HAVE DONE TO ME.
YOU HAVE DONE WELL. HERE IS BUT A TASTE OF THE GLORY THAT AWAITS YOU WHEN OUR BARGAIN IS FINISHED.
YES. OH, YES.

NOOOOO.

YOU MAY HAVE KILLED *BEOWULF* FOR THIS? YOU WOULD LET ALL OUR WORLDS *BURN?*
ALL THOSE AND A THOUSAND MORE!

HAHAHAHAHAHA!
PAIN! I CAN FEEL THE *PAIN!*
REGRET! GUILT!
IT IS *DELICIOUS!*

WELL, STALKER. IT LOOKS LIKE I MAY GET TO KEEP YOUR SOUL, AFTER ALL.

WHAT? THIS IS *NOTHING.* WE CAN STILL TAKE THEM *EASILY.*
WELL PLAYED, PRINCESS.

TEND TO BEOWULF IF YOU CAN, CLAW. DON'T LET HIM DIE A MEAL FOR THIS OBSCENITY.
...
YOU HAVE MY WORD.
PRINCESS.
SHE DIDN'T REALLY *BEAT* ME. I *LET* HER STRIKE ME. IT'S... IT'S SIMPLY THE NEW *SENSATION* THAT...
I WASN'T TRYING TO *HURT* YOU, STALKER.

I WAS TRYING TO *STEAL* FROM YOU.

AND BY THE *WAY*?

"ELPIS" IS A *GIRL'S* NAME.

NO. YOU CAN'T. NOOOOOO!

AND THE HORRIFIC THING FOR HIM?

HE ONCE AGAIN HAS THE ABILITY TO UNDERSTAND ***TORMENT.***

AS I HAVE REGAINED THE ABILITY TO UNDERSTAND ***SACRIFICE.***

WHAT?

YOU FOOL. WE'LL BOTH DIE!

THE SHARD. IT'S MY LODESTONE. IT WILL TAKE ME WHERE I MIGHT FIND ***REDEMPTION.***

ALL DEBTS SHALL BE WIPED CLEAN, OR I ***DIE*** *IN THE ATTEMPT.*

I ALMOST LOOK ***FORWARD*** *TO IT.*

I CURSE YOU, AMAZON! I CURSE YOUR PEOPLE!

OTHERS HAVE THREATENED MY PEOPLE BEFORE, DEVIL, AND I CAN *SENSE* YOUR POWER.

THE GAUNTLET. IT ***PROTECTS*** *ME FROM D'GRTH'S UNHOLY* ***FLAME.*** *IT'S ALMOST LIKE...*

...DESTINY.

BUT THE DIFFERENCE BETWEEN US NOW, D'GRTH?

SPPPLOOOOSHH

EVEN FOR THE STALKER.

THIS ENDS HERE.

AND YOU SHALL NEVER SEE ANOTHER DAWN.

WONDER WOMAN #23 Cover by Aaron Lopresti with Alex Sinclair

I HAVE BEEN DRAGGED THROUGH EVERY FORSAKEN DIMENSION AND LOCALITY.
MY BODY HAS BEEN INVADED AND ALTERED TO MAKE ME MORE FIT FOR THE GROTESQUE DUTY I HAVE BEEN CHOSEN TO ACCOMPLISH.

MY SOUL HAS BEEN STOLEN AND DIMINISHED, MY AFFINITY FOR MY OWN LASSO ABOLISHED BECAUSE OF IT.
AND MOST ANNOYINGLY, EVERY SWORDLACKEY AND WOULD-BE ASSASSIN ON THREE WORLDS HAS CALLED ME WHATEVER THE LOCAL SLANG IS FOR "STRUMPET."

LESS INSULTING BUT MORE PRESSINGLY, MY POWERS HAD BEEN ROUGHLY TAKEN JUST AS I FOUND MYSELF ON A QUEST TO KILL THE DEVIL.
D'GRTH, HE CALLS HIMSELF ON THE STALKER'S FLAT WORLD. THE WORLD OF THE BLACK HORIZON.

BUT THAT WAS THERE. THAT WAS THEN. THERE, I WAS DIANA.
AND HERE? ON MY WORLD?

HERE, I AM WONDER.
...STUNNING, HORRIFIC SPECTACLE, AS WONDER WOMAN, SCRATCH THAT, SOMEONE WHO LOOKS LIKE LIKE SHE MIGHT BE WONDER WOMAN, IS FACING WHAT I CAN ONLY DESCRIBE AS...SOME SORT OF DEMON OR MONSTER...
HEAVEN HELP US, IT LOOKS LIKE THE DEVIL HIMSELF!
WWDC NEWS
ENDS OF THE EARTH FINAL

WE APOLOGIZE FOR THE IMAGE QUALITY, LADIES AND GENTLEMEN, AS ERNIE SCHNEIDER, OUR TRAFFIC AND WEATHER EXPERT, IS QUITE UNDERSTANDABLY A LITTLE SHAKEN UP AT THIS SHOCKING TURN OF EVENTS.
NO, JAIME, I'M SERIOUS! I THINK IT'S THE DEVIL!
YOU HEAR ME? I THINK THIS IS JUDGMENT DAY!
WE'RE GOING TO-- WE'RE GOING TO TRY TO GET A CLOSER SHOT, JAIME...

GAPING, GAWKING IMBECILES.
I SHOULD LET THEM DIE IN FLAME AND CLAW.

GAAAAH!
LEAVE THE AREA, YOU FOOLS!
DO YOU NOT SEE WHAT LIES BELOW US?
TOO LATE.
GNATS AND NUISANCE.

UGHN!
AND THUS WE SEE THE DANGER OF MISTAKING A LUST FOR BASE TITILLATION WITH A LUST FOR TRUE KNOWLEDGE.
ONE BRINGS WISDOM, AND THE OTHER?
ONLY DEGRADATION.

SON OF A DUNG-EATING VERMIN.
TRAITOR!
WORLD'S END--STALKER'S HOMEWORLD.
YOU BETRAYED US. BECAUSE OF YOU, BEOWULF IS DYING AND THE WOMAN MIGHT ALREADY BE DEAD! I WON'T ABIDE A TRAITOR.
I'LL KILL YOU FOR THAT, STALKER!
Unnhr.
HON... HONESTLY, BARBARIAN?

I MOST SINCERELY WISH THAT YOU COULD.
UNTOLD THOUSANDS HAVE TRIED.

HE... CLAW, DON'T KILL HIM. YET.
HE... HASN'T TOLD US EVERYTHING.
YOU SEE MUCH, OH WARRIOR OF LEGEND.

PERHAPS THAT'S WHY YOU HAVE A POEM, AND I HAVE ONLY THE REMORSE OF MULTITUDES LEFT IN MY WAKE.
IT'S TRUE. I DID BETRAY DIANA. BUT I HAD A LITTLE ASSISTANCE IN THAT REGARD.
FELLOW SINNERS, I GIVE YOU THE HOSTESS OF THIS ROACH'S FEAST...

...ORACLE, THE WITCH QUEEN.
I BID YOU WELL, INSTRUMENTS OF OUR REVENGE, DEAR TOKENS, DEAR PAWNS.
LET US DISCUSS YOUR FIERY DEATHS, SHALL WE?
OH, DEAR. OH, DEAR.
WHY AREN'T WE DEAD? WHY AREN'T WE DEAD?
SHUT UP, ERNIE. JUST... JUST SHUT UP.
OH.
FOOLS.
MOVE OR BURN, GENTLEMEN.
THE CHOICE IS YOURS.
APPARENTLY A BIT OF WEAKNESS, OF MERCY, HAS YET TO BE PURGED FROM THE CAVERN WHERE MY SOUL USED TO RESIDE.
CAN'T BE HELPED.

YOU FACE A SIMILAR CHOICE, AMAZON.
I OFFER YOU THE HONOR OF BEING MY VASSAL. BY SERVING ME, YOU WILL ATTAIN ALL THE JUICE AND JOY THIS WORLD HAS TO OFFER. YOUR GODS WILL AGAIN BE WORSHIPPED.
YOUR SISTERS FOREVER FREE FROM WANT, WORRY, OR DISMAY.
MOVE TO ME, PRINCESS...

OR BECOME CINDER.
SO MUCH POWER.
WHAT I COULD DO.

WILL YOU LIVE, WARRIOR?
A... A MOMENT, LORD D'GRTH.
MY OWN LASSO, THE GIFT OF HEPHAESTUS, CAN'T FIND ME IN THE EMPTY SHELL I HAVE BECOME. MY LIFE AS A HERO, AS A SYMBOL, MIGHT BE OVER.
AND WHAT I COULD DO! FEED THE HUNGRY, COMFORT THE ORPHANED, PROTECT THE...

...THE WILDLIFE. THE WOLVES.
FROM BEOWULF'S TIME. THE WOLVES.

WELL? WHAT IS YOUR CHOICE, PRINCESS?

WHEN I BEGAN THIS STORY, LORD--I MET A PACK OF RABID WOLVES. EVERY MOMENT THEY CONTINUED TO LIVE ONLY INCREASED THEIR PAIN.

AND, A PACK TO THE END, THEY ASKED ME TO END THEIR LIVES, SO THAT THEY WOULDN'T ATTACK EACH OTHER BEFORE DYING.

I ASK YOU, AS ALL WHO FACE A GOD MUST, WHY SHOULD IT BE THAT THEY, WHO LIVED ONLY AS INSTINCT AND HONOR COMMANDED, DIE COLD, IN THE SNOW...

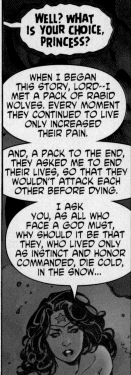

...WHILE A MURDERING SON-OF-A-JACKAL LIKE YOU LIVES ON?
GAAAAH!
OH, HERA.
FOR THE MOMENT, DEVIL.
JUST FOR THE MOMENT.
HIS FIRE--IT'S UNNATURAL.
INDESCRIBABLE.

YOUR REFUSAL IS NOTED, SPECK.
I SHALL SET THIS WORLD ASIDE FOR SPECIAL TORMENT ON YOUR BEHALF.
I'LL EAT YOUR PEOPLE LAST, GIRL.
VERY WELL, THEN.
IF IT'S DEATH BY FLAME, THEN AT LEAST LET THERE BE TWO ON THE PYRE, TODAY.
THIS CREATURE HAS FED OFF THE MISERY OF OTHERS FOR LONGER THAN THIS WORLD HAS BEEN. AND NOW IT HUNGERS FOR EVEN MORE.
PERHAPS I CAN AT LEAST SPOIL ITS APPETITE.
PERHAPS, EVEN WITHOUT MY SOUL...
...I CAN CHOOSE TO BE LIKE THE WOLF.

THE HOME OF DIANA PRINCE...
NEMESIS... AGENT TRESSER...
CAN I ASK HOW YOU PREFER TO BE ADDRESSED?

I DON'T KNOW, LADY.
HOWSABOUT YOU JUST CALL ME MR. GUY-WITH-A-RIFLE?
AS YOU LIKE.
YOU'RE NOT HURT, ARE YOU?
LET ME INTRODUCE MYSELF. MY NAME IS...
I KNOW WHO YOU ARE.

HE MEANT THE PRINCESS HARM. I KNOW IT. I SENSED THE SUSPICION!
HOLD, PLEASE, RHANDA.
IS THIS TRUE, MR. GUY-WITH-A-RIFLE?

...
MY BOSS. DIRECTOR STEEL. HE...
HE SAYS THERE'S A CONSPIRACY. HE SAYS THAT WHEN YOUR DIRECT MILITARY ATTACK DIDN'T WORK, YOU STARTED PLACING SLEEPERS IN HIGH GOVERNMENT AGENCIES.
SAID PRINCE AND CANDY WERE BOTH AMAZON SPOOKS.

I SEE. AND DO YOU BELIEVE HIM, AGENT TRESSER?
YEAH. I THINK IT'S POSSIBLE. MAYBE BEFORE THE ATTACKS ON D.C. I WOULDN'T HAVE BELIEVED IT, BUT...
I SEE.

DO YOU KNOW WHAT THESE ARE?
SURE I DO. AND MAYBE YOU CAN DEFLECT MY BULLETS, BUT JUST THE SAME...
NO, NEMESIS. THAT'S NOT THE FULL TRUTH OF THEIR POWER. THAT'S JUST THE FIREWORKS. THEIR MEANING IS ANOTHER THING ENTIRELY.
ONE MOMENT.

AGENT THOMAS TRESSER.
WITH THE BLOOD OF MY LIFE AND THAT OF MY SISTERS, I SWEAR TO YOU THAT I MEAN YOU NO HARM TO BODY OR SPIRIT. NOR WILL I ALLOW HARM TO COME TO YOU FROM ANY QUARTER, IF BY MEANS OF ANY MEASURE INCLUDING MY DEATH, I MAY PREVENT IT.
THIS I VOW AS SECOND CHILD OF THEMYSCIRA.

I CALL YOU MY FRIEND AND ALLY, TOM. WILL YOU HAVE ME?

MAN, WHAT IS IT WITH YOU PEOPLE AND MAKING ME FEEL LIKE A GRADE-A CHUMP ALL THE TIME?
MORE LIKE A MAN IN LOVE, I WOULD SAY.
MAYBE THEY'RE THE SAME THING, IN THE END.

YOU DESERVE ANSWERS, TOM. BUT THEY'RE NOT MINE TO GIVE.
I ASK ONLY THAT YOU GIVE MY SISTER THE CHANCE TO TELL YOU IN HER OWN TIME.
...
OKAY. I FEEL LIKE I'M IN THE MIDDLE OF THE WRONG SCREENPLAY, SOMEHOW. BUT OKAY. I CAN WAIT.
A BIT.

I KNOW SHE'S TAKEN A FANCY TO YOU, TOM. I WAS JUST TELLING NIGHTWING THAT SHE *DESPERATELY* NEEDS TO GET--
WAIT. WAIT, WE HAVEN'T *DONE* ANYTHING YET...!

--A BOYFRIEND. SHE NEEDS TO GET A BOYFRIEND, IS WHAT I WAS SAYING.
UH OH. YOUR D.M.A. FRIENDS?
OH, *MAN.*
AND I WAS SCHEDULED FOR A *PAY* RAISE, *TOO.*

UH...
FALSE ALARM, GUYS... NO MONKEYS HERE.
DMA
OH, DAMN.

UM. NO OOT-SHAY THE AGENT-AY, POR FAVOR! FALSE ALARM! EVERYONE OUT OF THE POOL!

HE ISN'T SUITABLE FOR THE PRINCESS. HE TAKES NOTHING SERIOUSLY.
ON THE CONTRARY, TOLIFHAR.
HE TAKES EVERYTHING INCREDIBLY SERIOUSLY.
AND HE CARRIES THAT WEIGHT ALONE.

OH.
CAN'T... CAN'T
ET HIM...
...SEE THE PAIN.

WHAT IS THAT, WARRIOR?
YOU SAY YOUR BRAVADO HAS BETRAYED YOU?

PERHAPS YOUR AVATAR HAS LED YOU ASTRAY?

I AM AGONY, GIRL.
YOU COULD NO MORE DEFEAT ME THAN YOU CAN DEFEAT DEATH. YOUR WOLF LIED TO YOU.

NO, DEVIL. HIS EXAMPLE *SAVED* ME.
NO MATTER WHAT DIMENSION IT'S LEFT IN, AN AMAZON'S SOUL IS HER *OWN.*
AND I HAVE ONE MORE BIT OF NEWS--

MY LASSO HAS *RETURNED* TO ME!

KRAAACK

I ALWAYS WONDERED...

...WHO DO THE GODS CALL TO IN THEIR TIME OF DESPAIR?

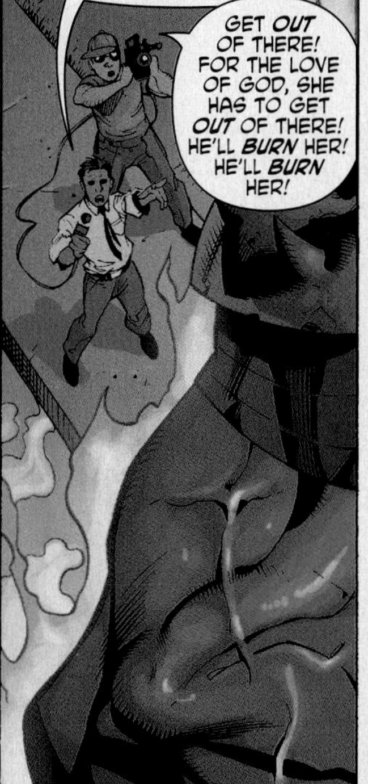

...DON'T KNOW WHAT TO SAY, JAMIE. THIS IS THE WOMAN THAT JUST A FEW MINUTES AGO SAVED OUR LIVES, AND SHE'S... SHE'S GOING TO BE...
GET OUT OF THERE! FOR THE LOVE OF GOD, SHE HAS TO GET OUT OF THERE! HE'LL BURN HER! HE'LL BURN HER!

YOU SCRATCHED ME.
NO LIVING THING HAS WOUNDED ME WITHOUT ETERNAL REGRET.

THEY GAVE ME THESE TOOLS TO DEFEAT YOU IN THIS WORLD. BUT AS IT TURNS OUT, ALL I NEEDED WAS WHAT I ALREADY HAD-- SOMETHING I HAVEN'T USED IN A WHILE.
AND AS RANKING DIPLOMAT OF THE ISLAND NATION OF THEMYSCIRA--

--I INVITE YOU TO GO STRAIGHT BACK TO HELL, DEMON!

SOME TIME LATER...
WE...WE CAN STILL MAKE A BARGAIN.
THAT TIME IS PAST.
YOU WON'T DO IT. YOU'RE NO MURDERER.
...
BE QUIET.
CLAW. SHE RETURNS
THE HELM-PRINCESS RETURNS!
HUSH.
WAIT. I OFFER YOU ALL KINGSHIPS. WORLDS OF CONQUEST. WHATEVER YOU WANT.
ALL YOU DREAM AND MORE.

THERE'S LITTLE TIME. HE'LL REGENERATE AND MAKE MORE MISCHIEF.
FOUR SWORDS AT ONCE. *YOUR* FOUR SWORDS, ON THE GREAT STONE TABLET, OR HE *LIVES* TO KILL *AGAIN.*
IT SEEMS YOU WON'T *NEED* TO BE MARTYRS, AFTER *ALL.*
I WON'T DO IT.
IF HE DIES, THEN... THEN...
I AM *AGAIN* IN THE *BLACKNESS ETERNAL!*
STALKER.
ELPIS.
THE SOUL YOU'RE WEARING-- IT'S NOT YOUR OWN. SEARCH YOUR HEART. D'GRTH CONSUMED THAT PART OF YOU EONS AGO.
MY SOUL HAD TO GO *SOMEWHERE.*
IT'S NOT *YOUR* SOUL YOU FEEL. IT'S *MINE.*
NO. *NO.*
IT WAS A GIFT OF THE GODS TO MY MOTHER AND TO ME, WARRIOR.
I CAN'T LET YOU HAVE IT.
I AM SORRY.
POWERFUL I MAY BE, BUT EVEN I CANNO UNDO THE BARGAINS O THE DEMON LORD.
STALKER SOUGHT HIS SOUL BACK, AND H THOUGHT GIVING THE THR OF YOU, YOU FIERCE-HEARTED WARRIORS T D'GRTH, HE WOULD GET IT.
WHEREF I?
I SOUG ONLY REVENG

IN THE END, THE ORACLE'S PROPHECY WAS RIGHT.
YOU HAVE BEEN CALLED MANY THINGS. YOU HAVE DONE MUCH THAT IS COLD-HEARTED, STALKER.
BUT YOU NEVER WERE CALLED A THIEF.
TAKE IT BACK, THEN.
TAKE IT BACK, DAMN YOU.
SHE SAID I WOULD REGRET MEETING THE STALKER 'TIL THE END OF MY DAYS.
THIS IS THE WORST THING I'VE EVER HAD TO DO TO ANOTHER HUMAN BEING. MURDER WOULD BE A MISDEMEANOR IN COMPARISON. TORTURE WOULD BE A LOVING EMBRACE.
THE PROPHECY WAS RIGHT.
THE DEMON MADE US SEVERAL MORE OFFERS, BARGAINS SO HIDEOUS AND UNGODLY THAT I SHALL NOT REPEAT THEM HERE.
HIS FINAL PLEADING WILL HAUNT ME FOREVER. IT WAS NOT MEANT FOR MORTAL EARS.
BUT FOR ALL HE HAD DONE, AND WHAT HE ASPIRED TO DO...
I LOWERED MY SWORD INTO THE EMPTY SOCKETS OF HIS EYES UNTIL I HIT THE LIVING MEAT UNDERNEATH.
AND THAT, I REGRET NOT AT ALL.
AND SO THE DEED IS DONE.

I CAN'T TAKE THIS, BEOWULF...

YOU CAN AND YOU WILL. I DON'T MEET EQUALS VERY OFTEN.

IT IS... AGREEABLE.

WITH THE POWER OF THE LODESTONE AND MY GIFT FROM KANE, I CAN SEND THEM HOME, AND YET SOMEHOW, WITH THE FIRE CRACKLING, I AM LOATH TO DO SO.

BEOWULF IS RIGHT. IT *IS* AGREEABLE.

THEY COULD ALMOST BE *AMAZONS.*

I WON'T SAY SUCH SWEET WORD PRINCESS. I IS NOT MY WAY.

BUT HAVE EITHER OF YOU NOTICED THAT *GRENDEL* SEEMS TO HAVE DISAPPEARED?

WELL, IT'S GOING TO BE A DEMOTION AND SUSPENSION AT LEAST, IF I'M *LUCKY.*

THE CONSEQUENCES OF DOING THE RIGHT THING AREN'T IMPORTANT. IT'S THE DEED THAT MATTERS.

OH, WELL, THAT SOLVES EVERYTHING.

HERE, I'VE MADE YOU TEA, HERO.

WHAT THE *HELL?*

RHANDA'S GROOMING YOU, TOM. I BELIEVE IT'S HIS WAY OF SHOWING ACCEPTANCE.

OKAY. THIS HAS OFFICIALLY GOTTEN WEIRD.

TOM... I NEED A STRAIGHT ANSWER HERE.
DO YOU LOVE DIANA?

RESPECTFULLY, STAR LADY... THAT'S OUR BUSINESS, HERS AND MINE.
...
I'M NOT AMAZON, MS. TROY. I HAVEN'T MADE A PRETTY SPEECH SINCE HIGH SCHOOL DEBATE. AND I LOST THAT ONE.
I CAN'T... I CAN'T EXPLAIN IT ANY BETTER THAN THAT.

I WOULD BE CONCERNED IF YOU COULD.
I GIVE MY APPROVAL.
GOODBYE, DEAR ONE. FOR MY SISTER'S SAKE, I HOLD YOU IN MY HEART.
BE BRAVE FOR THE TRIALS AHEAD.

AND WHATEVER YOU DO, DON'T UPSET HIPPOLYTA!

FOR THE LOVE OF GOD, WILL YOU QUIT PICKING AT MY SCALP?

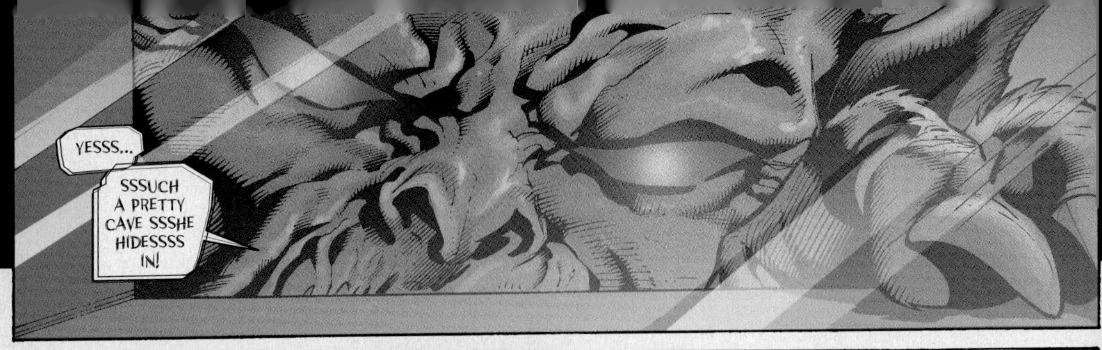
YESSS...
SSSUCH A PRETTY CAVE SSSHE HIDESSSS IN!

DIRECTOR STEEL'S OFFICE, DEPARTMENT OF METAHUMAN AFFAIRS.
TRESSER SAID IT WAS WHAT?
A FALSE ALARM, SIR.

HE SAID HE ACCIDENTALLY SET OFF A GRENADE AND SUFFERED MOMENTARY SHELL SHOCK.
NO, SIR, I'M SURE HE DIDN'T MEAN TO--
YES, SIR, I'LL BE SURE TO KEEP MY NEWBIE OPINIONS TO MYSELF, ABSOLUTELY, SIR.

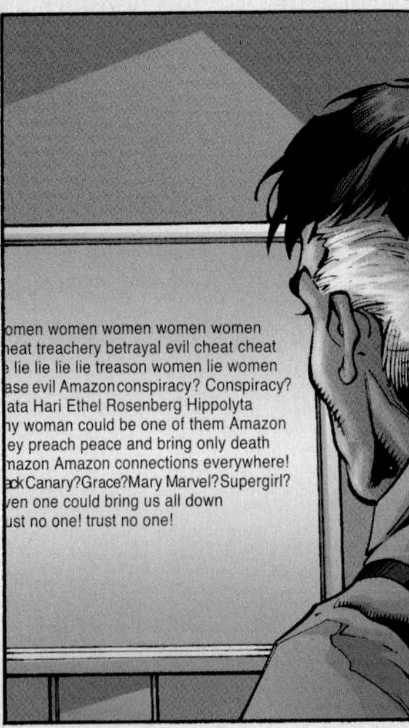
omen women women women women
heat treachery betrayal evil cheat cheat
e lie lie lie lie treason women lie women
ase evil Amazon conspiracy? Conspiracy?
ata Hari Ethel Rosenberg Hippolyta
ny woman could be one of them Amazon
ey preach peace and bring only death
mazon Amazon connections everywhere!
ack Canary?Grace?Mary Marvel?Supergirl?
ven one could bring us all down
ust no one! trust no one!

women women women women women
cheat treachery betrayal evil cheat cheat
Lie lie lie lie lie treason women lie women
Tease evil Amazon conspiracy? Conspiracy?
Mata Hari Ethel Rosenberg Hippolyta
Any woman could be one of them Amazon
They preach peace and bring only death
Amazon Amazon connections everywhere!
Black Canary? Grace? Mary Marvel? Superg
Even one could bring us all down
Trust no one! Trust no one!
Tom Tresser is working with them!!!

WONDER WOMAN #24
Cover by Aaron Lopresti with Hi-Fi

ARE YOU COLD?
I'M SORRY. I SOMETIMES FORGET ABOUT MORTAL COMFORTS.
HONESTLY?
I DON'T KNOW *HOW* I FEEL.
I GUESS I HAVE THER CONCERNS ENTIRELY, YOU KNOW?
LIKE OUR MODE OF--
LIKE OUR MODE OF TRANSPORT, YES.
IT'S OUR DESTINATION THAT TROUBLES ME.
THAT, TOO.
DON'T W WHAT SAY.
DON'T OW HOW O ACT.
THE ONLY SAFE APPROACH IS ABSOLUTE TRUTH, TOM.
NO HESITATION, NO EQUIVOCATION.
I KNOW YOU HIDE YOUR TRUE SELF, TOM. I UNDERSTAND THAT THAT'S NECESSARY IN YOUR LINE OF WORK.
I CAN HANDLE IT. I'M A MODERN WOMAN.

MY MOTHER IS A BIT MORE OLD-FASHIONED, HOWEVER.
THOMAS ANDREW TRESSER.
WARRIOR.
SPY.
A STAR IN TH
PART ONE OF TWO
WELCOME TO OUR HOME.
UH...
SHE'S SUMMONING YOU FORWARD, TOM.
NO, YEAH, I GOT THAT, BUT... UM...
I'M A GUY. DON'T GUYS BLOW UP OR SOMETHING IF THEY SET FOOT ON PARADISE ISLAND?
NOT LATELY, THOMAS ANDREW TRESSER.
WILL YOU KEEP A QUEEN WAITING FOREVER?

CLAIMANT OF MY DAUGHTER'S HEART.
WELCOME TO *THEMYSCIRA.*
HEAVENS
CELEBRITY
SORRY. SORRY!
I SAY AGAIN, WELCOME.
YOU HONOR US.
THANK YOU...
IT'S A PLEASURE TO BE HERE.
IS THAT SO?
IS IT *REALLY?*
NO.
NOT IN THE SLIGHTEST.

BUT IT *IS* AN HONOR, YOUR MAJESTY.
AND I'M SORRY-- I WASN'T QUITE PREPARED FOR YOU TO BE SO...
...SO BEAUTIFUL.
KINDLY AND PRECISELY SAID.
THE SUN RISES. THERE ARE CHORES TO BE DONE, AND NO SAVE US, TO DO THE WILL YOU AID ME, THOMAS?
I CAN HELP, MOTHER...
STAY, DAUGHTER.
THOMAS SEEMS *QUITE* CAPABLE.

THIS IS THE HOUSING FOR THE ROYAL MENAGERIE, THOMAS.
MANY BEASTS LIVE HERE THAT HAVE PASSED FROM THE REST OF THE WORLD.
THEY ARE SAFE HERE. CONTACT WITH THE OUTSIDE WOULD BE FATAL.
SO WE KEEP THEM HERE. NOT OUT OF CRUELTY.
OUT OF LOVE.
PEOPLE AREN'T ANIMALS, YOUR MAJESTY.
THAT IS SELF-EVIDENT.
PERHAPS MY WORDS MEANT NO LARGER PURPOSE.
BE AT EASE, WARRIOR.
EWW. THIS...WOW, THIS SMELLS--
REVOLTING. YES.
IT IS THE LEAVINGS OF LAST WEEK'S SLAUGHTER, LEFT TO ROT.
THE GRIFFINS PREFER IT THAT WAY.
I'VE SPOILED THEM.
THEY LIKE TO BE HAND-FED, NOW.
WELL, YOU KNOW HOW IT IS WITH *GRIFFINS.*

ARE THEY...?
OH, THEY'RE PERFECTLY SAFE. AS LONG AS YOU DON'T MAKE ANY SUDDEN MOVEMENTS. OR SWEAT.
AND I WOULDN'T MAKE EYE CONTACT, IF I WERE YOU.
THEY MATE FOR LIFE, YOU KNOW.
HAVE YOU MADE LOVE TO MY DAUGHTER, TOM?
PSSSHOO....!
WHAT?
SQUAAWREEEEEEEE
CEASE!
NOT FOOD. THIS MAN IS NOT FOOD.
THEY DON'T LIKE YOU. BREAKFAST CAN WAIT.
I'LL ASK A DIFFERENT WAY. HAVE YOU ATTEMPTED TO PROCREATE WITH MY DAUGHTER YET, TOM?
...NO. NO, WE HAVEN'T EVEN--
STOP.
THERE ARE FORMALITIES. NOTHING LIKE THIS HAS HAPPENED ON THIS ISLAND FOR...
...QUITE SOME TIME.

HAVE YOU BEEN WED BEFORE?
NO. I...
I HAVEN'T BEEN CLOSE TO ANYONE FOR A GOOD WHILE.
AS I MEASURE IT, ANYWAY.
WILL YOU PROTECT HER, KEEP HER FROM HARM, IF YOU ARE ABLE?
YES.
THAT I CAN PROMISE. ALTHOUGH IT USUALLY GOES THE OTHER WAY 'ROUND, TO BE BLUNT.
THERE IS ONLY ONE MORE QUESTION, THOMAS.
NOT AS PRINCESS, NOT FOR WHAT SHE CAN DO, BUT FOR WHO SHE TRULY *IS*--
--DO YOU LOVE HER?
I DO, YOUR MAJESTY.
I DO.
LOOK, I KNOW I DON'T BELONG HERE. I KNOW YOU THINK I'M NOT WORTHY.
I THINK NOTHING OF THE KIND.
THIS IS FOR YOU.
I MADE IT FOR *YOUR* HAND.

ORDINARILY, THERE WOULD BE AN APPROVAL PARTY. BUT MY TRIBE...
...THEY ARE TEMPORARILY LOST.
YOU WILL NEED A TITLE AND RANK.
I CALL YOU GUARDSMAN, AND HERE YOU SHALL BE SIR THOMAS, OF...?
CLEVELAND.
CLEVELAND.
I LIKE IT. IT SOUNDS LIKE A WARRIOR'S HOMELAND.
A GOOD PORTENT.
THAT'S IT?
I THOUGHT IT'D BE A LIFE AND DEATH BATTLE OVER A FLAMING PIT OF SNAKES OR SOMETHING.
WHO IS TO SAY THAT IT WAS NOT?
YOU ARE AN AMAZON NOW, THOMAS.
NO MATTER WHAT HAPPENS FROM NOW ON, YOU MUST NEVER FORGET THAT.
YOU MUST BE TRUE TO YOUR SISTERS. FOR ANY OF US WOULD GIVE OUR LIFE FOR YOU WITHOUT A MOMENT'S HESITATION.
YOU HAVE MY APPROVAL, DIANA. I WISH YOU ONLY HAPPINESS.
RETURN TO HIS WORLD WITH MY BLESSING.
MOTHER...
HUSH.
I WANT ONLY ONE MORE THING FROM YOU, SIR THOMAS OF CLEVELAND.
WHATEVER YOU WANT, YOUR MAJESTY.
BABIES, GOOD GUARDSMAN.
AS MANY AS YOU CAN PROVIDE FOR, AS QUICKLY AS YOU MAY PRODUCE THEM.
BABIES, BABIES, BABIES.
I DON'T THINK SHE LIKED ME.
ULTIMATELY, IT'S MY DECISION, TOM.
YOU MEAN *OUR* DECISION, RIGHT?

YES. OUR DECISION. I'M NOT USED TO THINKING LIKE THAT.
IT'S A LOT TO ABSORB, DIANA. YOU'VE WITHSTOOD NUCLEAR EXPLOSIONS. YOU'VE STOOD IN HOT LAVA.
I MEAN, CAN YOU EVEN...
CAN YOU EVEN *FEEL* THIS?
...
NO, TOM.
NOT THE WAY *YOU* DO, I'LL ADMIT.
BUT I DO FEEL *SOMETHING.*
I'M SORRY IF SHE SCARED YOU. SHE DOES HAVE THAT ABILITY.
ME? SCARED? PFFT.
I'M NOT SCARED *YET,* PRINCESS.
REALLY.
HERE... THESE ARE THE WATERS OF THE ISLAND YOU MIGHT RULE ONE DAY.
IT'S TRADITION TO IMMERSE YOUR RIGHT HAND.
FOR LUCK.
I REALLY DON'T SEE MYSELF RULING MUCH, DIANA.
ALL MY GOLDFISH DIE AND MY HOUSEPLANTS LOOK LIKE...

$%!#!!!

WHAT THE *HELL* WAS *THAT?*

THEY GUARD OUR WATERS. YOU *MUST* BE A TRUE AMAZON NOW, TOM.

WHAT?

WELL, HE DIDN'T *EAT* YOU, DID HE?

KIND OF A *MEAN* STREAK, HAVE WE?

AMAZON MATING PLAY.

IT'S NOT FOR THE WEAK.

FUNNY, HE DIDN'T *LOOK* LIKE HE LIKED ME.

PERHAPS HE HEARD ABOUT THE WAY YOU TEND YOUR GOLDFISH?

I'M DROPPING YOU OFF IN D.C., TOM, IF THAT'S ALL RIGHT.

SO SOON? I THOUGHT WE MIGHT SPEND...

I'M AFRAID I HAVE BUSINESS ON THE WEST COAST.

FRANKLY, I MIGHT SOONER FIGHT THE SHARKS.
METAPHORICAL SIMILARITY DULY NOTED, OF COURSE.
OLLYWO

CAN'T BELIEVE IT, IT'S JUST SO, SO, WHAT'S THE WORD?
UNBELIEVABLE?
YES.
HAD A PAIR OF HER BRACELETS FOR YEARS 'TIL I SOLD 'EM ON EPAY.
WAIT'LL SHE MEETS LANEY. SHE WON'T KNOW WHAT HIT HER. DOCTOR PSYCHO'S GONNA SEEM LIKE A GIRL SCOUT.
I'VE DEALT WITH THEIR LIKE BEFORE. THEY TEND TO BE VERY SINCERE AND WELL-INTENTIONED, AND CAUTIOUSLY KIND TO STRANGERS.

BUT THEY UNDERSTAND MY LIFESTYLE EVEN LESS THAN I UNDERSTAND THEIRS.
SECURITY SAYS SHE'S HERE, MS. KIRSWEL!
SHE IS VISITING ROYALTY, CHERRI. THE LEAST WE CAN DO IS OFFER HER SOMETHING TO DRINK, DON'T YOU THINK?
RIGHT AWAY, MA'AM!

I HAVE NOTHING BUT RESPECT FOR THE CREATIVE MIND.
THEN LET'S GET ON THAT, DEAR, SHALL WE?
RIGHT AWAY, MA'AM!

OKAY, DON'T MESS THIS UP, CHERRI. DO NOT CURTSEY, DO NOT SHAKE HER HAND, JUST A POLITE, SHORT BOW, AND THEN ASK IF SHE NEEDS...
WAIT, ASK FIRST IF SHE NEEDS ANYTHING, THEN THE POLITE, SHORT BOW...NO, WAIT.
I HOPE ALL THIS FORMALITY ISN'T FOR MY SAKE.
I EVEN RESPECT THE RAW, ENDLESS AMBITION.

OH, MY.
A PLEASURE TO MEET YOU, SISTER.
AND ONE SMALL THING I'VE LEARNED FROM DEALING WITH THEM IN THE PAST...

ALWAYS NEGOTIATE FROM A POSITION OF STRENGTH.
MY NAME IS DIANA. I BELIEVE I HAVE AN APPOINTMENT?
GUH.
UM...
I SWALLOWED MY GUM.
PRINCESS, IT'S A PLEASURE TO...
PLEASE CALL ME DIANA. MS. KIRSWEL.
THESE ARE MY TRUSTED ADVISORS, TOLIFHAR AND RHANDA.
THEY ARE SUPER-INTELLIGE AMBASSADOR FROM GORILLA CITY.
HMMFH.
AND SUCH DISTINGUISHED FELLOWS THEY ARE. STRIKING!
IT IS AS YOU SAY.
WE ARE MOST HANDSOME.
CHARMING. CHERRI?
ON IT.
YES. HMMM.
PLEASE, YOU MUST ALL CALL ME LANEY.
WHAT DID SHE TASTE LIKE?
UNPLEASANT.
I'M STILL NO COMPLETEL MYSELF FRO MY EXPERIEN WITH THE BLA HORIZON. PART OF THA VOID LINGER WITHIN ME.

BUT I RETAIN ENOUGH INSIGHT TO KNOW THAT THIS IS A POWERFUL WOMAN, DESPITE HER SMILE AND GRACE.
LET ME INTRODUCE THE TEAM ON THIS PROJECT, DIANA, SHALL I?
DENNY HERE IS OUR DIRECTOR, IT'S HIS VISION WE'RE TRYING TO CONVEY.
CROSS HERE IS OUR GIFTED WRITER--HE DID GRAVESTONE GRAVES, DID YOU HAPPEN TO CATCH... NO?
AND THIS IS ALLISON CONDERO, SHE'S REPRESENTING OUR LEGAL DEPARTMENT TODAY, YOU DON'T MIND IF SHE TAKES A FEW NOTES, YES?
BEWARE, DIANA.

PLEASE, PRINCESS. WE'RE ALL FRIENDS HERE. TAKE A SEAT, WON'T YOU?
MS. KIRSW... LANEY.
IT'S MY UNDERSTANDING THAT YOU INTEND TO MAKE THIS MOVIE OF MY LIFE WITH OR WITHOUT MY CONSENT, IS THAT CORRECT?
CAN I GET YOU ANYTHING, DIANA? ESPRESSO, MAYBE A NICE PLATE OF FRESH FRUIT?
NO THANK YOU, CHERRI.

IT'S LIKE THIS, DIANA. YES, YOUR LIFE IS PUBLIC KNOWLEDGE, BUT--
--BUT IF I WERE TO STATE MY UNHAPPINESS--
--IT WOULD HURT THE PICTURE, POSSIBLY. YES.

WE TOTALLY RESPECT THE WHOLE AMAZON THING, PRINCESS.
WE REALLY WANT TO MAKE A MOVIE YOU CAN BE PROUD OF.
ALLISON, TELL HER.
...
FINE.

YOU ENDORSE THE FILM.
YOU GET A CONSULTANT CREDIT.
WE DONATE A MILLION DOLLARS AND BACK-END POINTS TO THE ATHENIAN WOMAN'S HELP SHELTERS.

WHAT DO YOU TWO THINK?

...
WE WOULD LIKE TO HEAR MORE ABOUT THIS FRESH FRUIT PORTION OF THE NEGOTIATIONS.

CHERRI?
ON IT, BOSS!
SERIOUSLY, PRINCESS. WE WANT TO TELL A THRILLING ADVENTURE STORY, SOMETHING THAT'LL BE A TRUE INSPIRATION TO YOUNG GIRLS...
Snort!

YOU'LL HAVE TO FORGIVE ALLISON, DIANA. SHE'S...SHE DOESN'T QUITE SEE EYE-TO-EYE WITH THE REST OF US ON THIS.
PLEASE, SPEAK YOUR MIND, SISTER. I FEEL YOUR DOUBT.
ALL RIGHT. FINE.

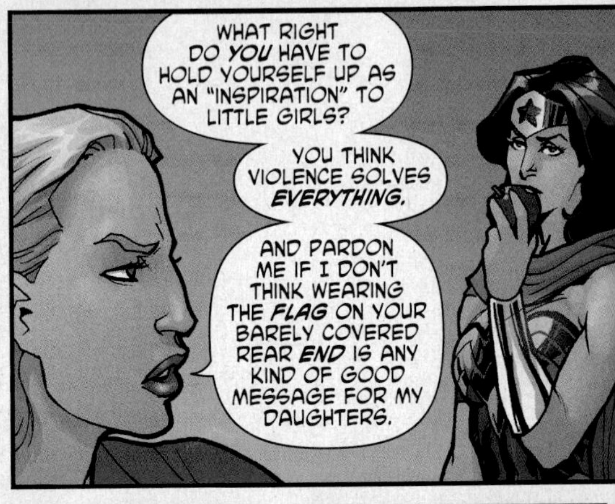
WHAT RIGHT DO YOU HAVE TO HOLD YOURSELF UP AS AN "INSPIRATION" TO LITTLE GIRLS?
YOU THINK VIOLENCE SOLVES EVERYTHING.
AND PARDON ME IF I DON'T THINK WEARING THE FLAG ON YOUR BARELY COVERED REAR END IS ANY KIND OF GOOD MESSAGE FOR MY DAUGHTERS.

IT'S NOT A FL--
THESE COLORS HAVE MEANING FOR ME, ALLISON.
AND WOULD YOU RATHER I BE ASHAMED OF MY BODY?

HEY. YOU ASKED. YOU WANT TO LOOK LIKE A STRIPPER, YOU BE MY GUEST.
ALLISON!
I WONDER...
I WONDER IF I MIGHT HAVE A MOMENT ALONE WITH MS. CONDERO, PLEASE.

GIRL CHAT. GOT IT.
WHEN YOU WORK IT OUT, PLEASE FEEL FREE TO JOIN US ON SET.
BOTH OF YOU. THAT'S AN ORDER, LADIES!

LOOK. YOU DON'T HAVE TO WORRY. I WAS OUTVOTED. THEY'LL MAKE YOUR SILLY MOVIE AND THEY'LL TRY TO KEEP YOU MOLLIFIED.
SURELY YOU'LL ALLOW ME TO HAVE MY OWN OPINIONS ON WHETHER OR NOT I THINK GLORIFYING YOU IS GOOD FOR CHILDREN?
I DON'T CARE ABOUT THAT, ALLISON. THAT'S NOT WHY I WANTED TO SPEAK WITH YOU.

WHAT...?
WAIT. WHAT ARE YOU...
HUSH, SISTER.

IT'LL BE ALL RIGHT IF YOU STOP NOW.
WHAT?

YOU...YOU DON'T KNOW.
I HAVE NO IDEA WHAT YOU'RE TALKING ABOUT!
I THINK YOU DO, ALLISON.

I CAN HELP.
STAY AWAY.
I HAVE NO PROBLEMS.
JUST STAY AWAY!

SLAM

WHAT DID YOU PUT IN YOUR BRIEFCASE?
NEWSPAPERS AND A SHOE. YOURS?
ROTTEN VEGETABLES, MOSTLY.
YES. YES, YES, YES.

YEAH, SEE, WE DON'T SKIP OVER THE DARK STUFF, PRINCESS. I KEEP TRYING TO CONVINCE THEM THAT WE SHOULD BE DOING *TWO* MOVIES BACK TO *BACK.*
BUT MAN, WE GOT *PATHOS* COMIN' OUT OUR--
SORRY. THIS IS MOSTLY JUST REHEARSAL STUFF, HERE.
SO WHAT WAS IT *REALLY* LIKE, DIANA... THAT TIME YOU FINALLY FACED *HIM?*
HERCULES?
"WE SHOULD NOT FIGHT, DIANA. JOIN ME, *HERCULES,* AND WE CAN DEFEAT CIRCE *TOGETHER!*"
"I CANNOT LOVE A MAN UNLESS HE FIRST *DEFEATS ME IN BATTLE!*"
"SO *BE* IT, BEAUTIFUL ONE!"
"I'M THOUSANDS OF YEARS TOO OLD FOR THIS *&^%!!!!"
NOT...
IT WAS NOT LIKE *THAT.*
YEAH, OKAY, *THAT* PART WE HAD TO FIX A LITTLE. THERE IS JUST A *TEENY* LOVE TRIANGLE...
IT'S *VERY* TASTEFUL.
"HOW IS IT THAT YOU HAVE DEFEATED ME, AND YET I'VE NEVER FELT MORE A WOMAN?"
"YOU THINK YOU FEEL LIKE A WOMAN NOW, WAIT'LL YOU SEE WHAT COMES *NEXT!*"
AND WE THINK *THAT'S* GONNA GET A *HUGE* LAUGH!

WHO IS IN THIS "TRIANGLE," CROSS?
WHY... IT'S YOU, HERCULES...
AND THE QUEEN, OF COURSE... HIPPOLYTA.
...NO.

DO YOU KNOW? DO YOU KNOW WHAT HE DID TO MY MOTHER?
DO YOU KNOW WHAT HE ALMOST DID TO THE ENTIRE WORLD?
YEAH, BUT... BUT... THAT DIDN'T TEST WELL!
THIS FILM IS CANCELED. IT'S OVER.

I SHOULD NEVER HAVE ALLOWED...
DIANA! DEAR, LISTEN, WE CAN ADJUST THE SCRIPT!
DO YOU THINK THESE THINGS ARE UNIMPORTANT?
TRUTH, AND LIBERTY... YOU THINK THEY DON'T MATTER?
THAT'S MY MOTHER'S LIFE YOU'RE MOCKING! YOU'VE TURNED HER FORCED TORMENT INTO LOVE.

I WILL NOT HAVE IT. I WILL FIGHT YOU.

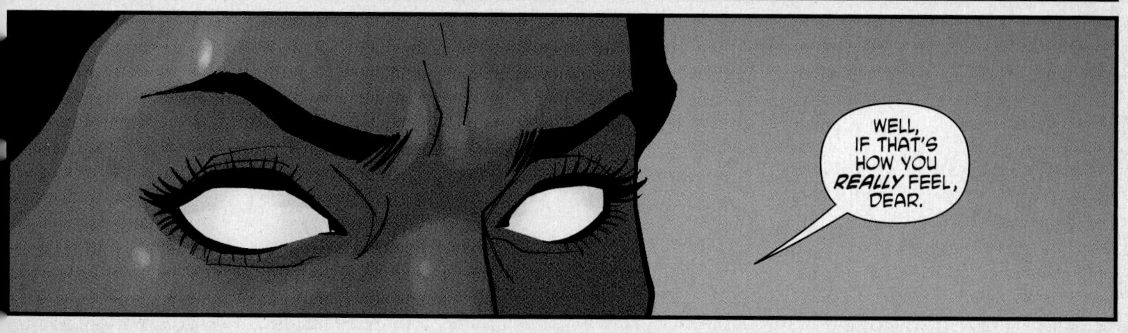
WELL, IF THAT'S HOW YOU REALLY FEEL, DEAR.

UGNNHH!
IMPOSTOR!

WE FIGHT *BESIDE* YOU, YOUR MAJESTY!

I'LL PUMMEL YOU INTO YOUR *TOMB*, FRAUD!
NO ONE PRETENDS TO BE *DIANA*.
I...
GHUHH--
I WAS, PERHAPS, NOT MEANT FOR THIS BUSINESS.

IT MIGHT BE TOO CUTTHROAT FOR ME.
UGHNN!

OH, IT REALLY IS TOO, TOO DELICIOUSLY DECADENT.
ALL THE SINS COME HOME, PRINCESS. THIS IS ONE THING I KNOW ABOUT THE UNIVERSE.
ALL SINS COME HOME, EVENTUALLY.

AH AH AH, DARLING.
DON'T MAKE ME USE MY *JUDO* ON YOU!
UGGGNN!

STILL WANT TO FIGHT?
WELL, *BEWARE* MY *CLAWS,* KITTEN!

IS THERE NO SENSE OF *ACCURACY* IN THIS PRODUCTION?
AAAUHH!

I WOULDN'T BE CAUGHT *DEAD* SPEAKING LIKE THAT.

MS. *KIRSWEL.* WHAT THE HELL IS GOING *ON???*
SHE'S HAD A *LOT* OF DEMONS TO FIGHT, CHERRI, DEAR.
MANY, *MANY* DARK NIGHTS OF THE SOUL.
WHAT CAN I SAY? IF SHE DIDN'T *WANT* TO BE MY TORTURED AND BATTERED PLAYTHING FOR ALL ETERNITY...

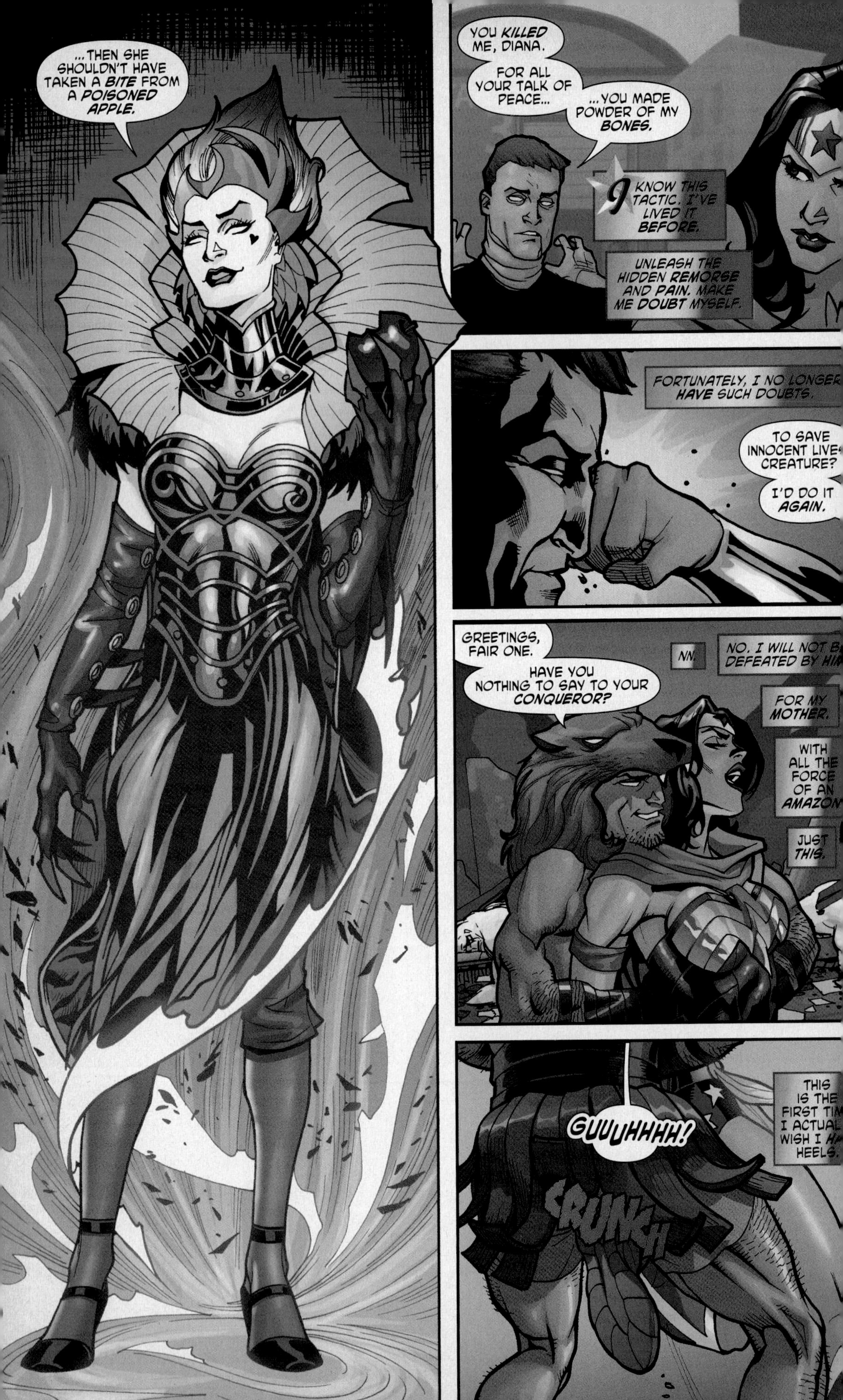
...THEN SHE SHOULDN'T HAVE TAKEN A BITE FROM A POISONED APPLE.
YOU KILLED ME, DIANA.
FOR ALL YOUR TALK OF PEACE...
...YOU MADE POWDER OF MY BONES.
I KNOW THIS TACTIC. I'VE LIVED IT BEFORE.
UNLEASH THE HIDDEN REMORSE AND PAIN. MAKE ME DOUBT MYSELF.
FORTUNATELY, I NO LONGER HAVE SUCH DOUBTS.
TO SAVE INNOCENT LIVES CREATURE?
I'D DO IT AGAIN.
GREETINGS, FAIR ONE.
HAVE YOU NOTHING TO SAY TO YOUR CONQUEROR?
NN.
NO. I WILL NOT B DEFEATED BY HIM
FOR MY MOTHER.
WITH ALL THE FORCE OF AN AMAZON
JUST THIS.
GUUUHHHH!
CRUNCH
THIS IS THE FIRST TI I ACTUAL WISH I H HEELS.

IN REPOSE.
FEEL FREE TO
ET UP AGAIN, COWARD,
ND I'LL HAPPILY SHOW
U WHAT MAX LEARNED,
TO HIS REGRET.
GLLLLPHHH!
SOMETHING'S WRONG.
STARTING TO THINK OF THESE... THESE POWERFUL MAGICS AS THE PEOPLE THEY REPRESENT.
POISON.
OH.
KEEP FILMING. FOR THE LOVE OF ALL THAT'S HOLY, YOU KEEP HER IN SHOT!
WHAT ARE YOU DOING? WHAT ARE YOU DOING TO WONDER WOMAN!?
THAT'S NOT HER REAL NAME, YOU KNOW. HER REAL NAME IS SNOW WHITE.
AND SHE OWES ME CENTURIES OF AGONY!
OH.

"BUT NO ONE SAID SHE HAD TO LIVE OUT THOSE EONS--
"--WITH ALL HER LIMBS ATTACHED!"

WONDER WOMAN #25 Cover by Aaron Lopresti with Hi-Fi

"OKAY, OKAY, HERE'S THE NEW PLAN. WE START WITH A CRANE SHOT...
"WON'T THAT COST A BUNDLE, DENNY?"
"NO, NO, WAIT... A *HELICOPTER* SHOT!"
"ARE YOU KIDDING? YOU BRING ME *MONEY* TALK WITH THIS?
"WE'RE TALKING THE *DEATH OF WONDER WOMAN,* HERE, IGGY! IT'S... I DON'T KNOW, IT'S *ICONIC* OR SOMETHING!"
"YOU'RE SUCH A *DOWNER,* IGGY.
"BUT WHAT IF, AND I'M JUST SAYING HERE... WHAT IF SHE DON'T *DIE?*"
"CLOSER, CAMERA TWO CLOSER... CLOSER..."
"I CAN'T *GET* NO..."
"CLOSER, CLOSER!
"TOO CLOSE! TOO CLOSE!"

IS...THERE'S THE MONEY SHOT!"
"I THINK MY NODE IS BUDDED."
"YOU'RE SUCH A DOWNER, IGGY."
A STAR IN THE HEAVENS SCENE 2: PERSONAL EFFECTS

WHAT... WHAT'S
PPENING? LANEY,
WHAT ARE YOU
DOING?
I SHOULD THINK IT WOULD BE OBVIOUS, CHERRI, DEAR.
LAST-MINUTE REWRITES.
BUT THAT... THAT'S WONDER WOMAN.
"WONDER WOMAN"?
NO.
THAT NAME IS A LIE. TO CONFUSE YOU ALL.
HER NAME IS SNOW WHITE.
I CAN'T HAVE AN ASSISTANT WHO MAKES MISTAKES LIKE THAT, DEAR.
YOU'RE FIRED.
NO NEED TO CLEAN OUT YOUR DESK, CHILD.

IT'S HER.
SHE'S BACK.
THE WICKED STEPMOTHER. THE BLACK EMPRESS.
THE DOWAGER OF SORROW. THE WELLSPRING OF ALL VILLAINESSES.
THE QUEEN OF FABLES.
AND HER TASTE FOR MISERY HAS RETURNED AS WELL.
HERMES HELP ME!
"...WHO ART IN HEAVEN, HALLOWED BE THY NAME, THY KINGDOM COME..."
THE SLIGHTEST MISCALCULATION AND THAT POOR GIRL IS DEAD.
ANOTHER NAME ON THE QUEEN'S TALLY.

AND TODAY, HER BILL HAS COME DUE.
WOOOF!
WHAT? I'M ALIVE?
YES. I'M SORRY IF MY COMING HERE PUT YOU IN DANGER, CHERRI.
...ARE YOU AN ANGEL?
WHAT?
NO, CHERRI. I'M NOT.
I PRAYED FOR YOU AND YOU CAME.
MAYBE YOU ARE AND YOU JUST DON'T KNOW IT.
UM...
THAT IS A COMPLICATED PROPOSITION.
SISTER.
IT'S OKAY.
I'M NOT AFRAID.
NOT THE FIRST TIME SOMEONE'S MADE THAT MISTAKE.
I MUST SAY IT'S FLATTERING.
THANK YOU FOR SENDING HER, LORD.

I'VE FOUGHT WITH HER BEFORE.
SHE ACTUALLY IS THE NIGHTMARE FROM THE CHILDREN'S FABLES OF AN UNTOLD NUMBER OF WORLDS. THE UNCENSORED AND HORRIFYING KIND, NOT THE KIND WE SEE IN ANIMATED FILMS.
SHE'S ALWAYS SEEN EVERYTHING THROUGH THE EYES OF HER STORIES. SHE HAS UNTOLD PRINCES AND CINDER-MAIDS AMONG HER MOST HATED PRESENCES.
SHE'S COMING. PROTECT YOUR QUEEN!
AND OF ALL THE CHARACTERS, ON EVERY WORLD, SHE HATES ONE MOST OF ALL.
THE PRINCESS. RAVEN HAIR AND RUBY LIPS.
THE GIRL WHO MADE HER DANCE IN IRON SHOES HOT FROM THE FIRE.
SNOW WHITE. THE PERSON SHE BELIEVES ME TO BE.
I'VE LEARNED TO MY REGRET THAT YOU CAN'T REALLY KILL HER.
LET'S SEE IF I CAN'T SOMEHOW SHOW HER I'M A DIFFERENT KIND OF PRINCESS ENTIRELY.
ENOUGH. YOU COULD HAVE KILLED THAT GIRL!
OH, SNOW WHITE. YOU KNOW SO LITTLE OF WHAT MAKES A GOOD TELLING.
AT THE BEGINNING OF MY TIME, OR NOW, EVERYONE KNOWS...

NO ONE CARES IF THE BLOOD OF AN INCIDENTAL PLAYER IS SPILT.
IT MERELY SWEETENS THE PERIL'S PERFUME.
I SEE YOU HAVEN'T CHANGED ANY, DARLING.
STILL THE UGLY SPOILED BRAT YOU'VE ALWAYS BEEN!
I HAVEN'T TIME FOR YOUR WARPED VIEW OF REALITY, QUEEN TSARITSA.
BEFORE I USE THIS ON YOU, I WANT TO HEAR IT FROM YOUR LIPS.
HOW DID YOU MAKE ALL THIS HAPPEN? WHAT HAPPENED TO THE REAL LANEY KIRSWEL?
OH, THAT IS A SAD TALE. EATEN BY A BIG, BAD WOLF, I BELIEVE.
THINK OF IT, SNOW... I AM THE MISTRESS OF TALES, AND WHO IN ALL THE LANDS TELLS MORE TALES THAN THESE PEOPLE?
WHY SHOULDN'T I COMMAND THEM? I'VE EVEN LEARNED SOME NEW WORDS, LIKE...
...CUT.

WHAT JUST HAPPENED?
THEY MUST NEVER KNOW... MY SISTERS MUST NEVER KNOW!
I HAVE BROKEN THE LAWS OF LOVE-- THEY WOULD NOT UNDERSTAND!
IS THIS... THIS WOMAN SUPPOSED TO BE MY MOTHER?
LISTEN, WHOEVER YOU ARE... YOU MUSTN'T DO THIS.
MY MOTHER IS A LIVING BEING. YOU HAVE NO RIGHT TO...
OH! BUT THE PAIN IN MY HEART SAYS THAT I AM COMMITTING A SIN! YOU MUST NEVER KNOW, DIANA... YOU MUST NEVER KNOW, FOR YOUR OWN SAKE...
...THE NAME OF YOUR TRUE FATHER!
OH, MY GODDESS.
THIS THING IS GOING TO BE THE BIGGEST BOMB IN FILM HISTORY.

WONDER WOMAN: THE MOVIE, SCENE 12, TAKE ONE!

Wonder Woman the Movie
12 Amazon Council scene
1 take

WHAT MANNER OF ABSURDITY?

QUEEN MOTHER, I WANNA GO PLAY WIF TH' UNYCORNS AGAIN!

WHAT IS IT, MAMA?

HUSH, DAUGHTER. YOU ARE OF AN AGE TO LEARN THE MOST *DANGEROUS* OPPONENT OUR PEOPLE FACE!

THIS WON'T BE GOOD.

THE PRINCESS WISHES TO KNOW THE FOULEST, BLOOD-THIRSTIEST AND MOST *DESTRUCTIVE* BEAST OF *ALL?*

WOULD *YOU*, THE ONLY *CHILD* OF *PARADISE ISLAND...*

...DARE TO FACE THAT WHICH IS THE *BANE* OF OUR VERY *EXISTENCE?*

MOTHER, I'M *FRIGHTENED!*

BE BRAVE, CHILD. REMEMBER YOUR *STATION.*

FOR I SAY UNTO *YOU...*

...THAT BEAST IS *MAN!*

LOOK! LOOK, CHILD! SEE ITS HORRIBLE *LUST!*

ITS *HUNGER* FOR *RAW MEAT* AND *ALCOHOL* AND *SEX!*

AND HERE I DIDN'T EVEN KNOW I WAS *CAPABLE* OF HAVING A MIGRANE.

WHY IS IT THAT PEOPLE FEEL THAT A BELIEF IN WOMEN EQUALS A HATRED OF MEN?
I CAN'T LOOK.
MOTHER, IS IT TRUE? DO THESE MONSTERS... THESE "MEN..."
ARE THEY REALLY THAT BAD?
THAT BAD AND MORE, PRINCESS!
THEY LOVE WAR! THEY AND WORST OF ALL--THEIR WOMEN!
AND WORST OF ALL--
PLEASE DON'T SAY IT, PLEASE DON'T SAY IT...
...THEY LEAVE THE TOILET SEATS UP!
KILL THE MEN! KILL THE MEN! KILL THE MEN!
URGH.
KILL THE SCREENWRITER, IS WHAT I SAY.
WELL, THIS IS A DIPLOMATIC NIGHTMARE.
THE WORLD ALREADY FEARS MY PEOPLE.
HAIR IN PLACES TOO TERRIBLE TO CONTEMPLATE! HORRID SMELLS! BEWARE THE SMELLS!
I NEVER WANT TO SEE A MAN, MOTHER! NEVER! DON'T LET THEM GET ME!
DON'T WORRY, CHILD. IF A MAN EVER TRIES TO EVEN COME NEAR YOU...
...I'LL TURN THEM FROM MAN TO WOMAN IN NO TIME!
SUDDENLY, REOPENING A CHAPTER OF THE JUSTICE LEAGUE ANTARCTICA SOUNDS LIKE A WISE AND REASONED PLAN.
THE SMELLS ARE EVERYWHERE!

WHAT CATASTROPHE IS THIS SCENE GOING TO BE?
ALARM! ALARM!
THERE IS AN INTRUDER!
I WILL SAY THAT THIS "PARADISE ISLAND" LOOKS SUSPICIOUSLY LIKE PARTS OF THE MALIBU COASTLINE...
STAND AWAY, DIANA! YOU DON'T KNOW WHAT THAT... THAT BEAST IS CAPABLE OF!
BUT MOTHER!
I LOVE HIM!
HE'S EVIL, DAUGHTER! I ORDER YOU TO STAND ASIDE!
BUT MOTHER, HOW CAN THERE BE EVIL...
...INSIDE OF SOMETHING SO...SO BEAUTIFUL?
DID A STAR FALL FROM HEAVEN AND MAKE YOU, PRINCESS?
OH, NO. WHAT WILL STEVE THINK?
WHAT WILL ETTA THINK?
OKAY. ENOUGH.
ENOUGH.
DO YOU THINK I WILL STAND BY AND SIMPLY OBSERVE WHILE YOU SLANDER MY PEOPLE AND MY LOVED ONES?
DO YOU THINK I WON'T STOP YOU?

IT'S NO FUN UNLESS SHE PARTICIPATES.

"DEAR HORRID GIRL, I GIVE YOU THE CONTEST."

THE CENTAURS AND I NEVER REALLY GOT ALONG.
TWO-LEGS, TWO-LEGS, CARVE THE WHITE MEAT FOR A TROPHY PLATE!

MISSED AGAIN, DANDY FORELOCK!
THAT WAS MEAN.
THEY HATE TO BE CALLED THAT.

LET'S TAKE THIS BATTLE'S MEASURE.

ARMS BOUND TIGHTLY BY SOME TWISTED VERSION OF MY OWN LASSO...

TWO MYSTICALLY POWERED BEINGS WITH A LUST FOR MY BLOOD, AND MAGIC AXES FROM HEPHAESTUS HIMSELF...

OH, GO COOK ME A COUPLE OF ORPHANS IN A PIE, YOU EMPTY SUITCASE.
AT ONCE, YOUR MAJESTY.
WE'RE GOING TO SKIP AHEAD A BIT, SNOW WHITE. I HOPE YOU DON'T MIND, BUT I DO DEARLY LOVE THIS SECTION.
IT'S TESTING WELL WITH ALL THE RIGHT DEMOS.
UH, OH.
WELL, SHE GOT ONE SMALL DETAIL RIGHT.
AND A PHALANX OF AMAZONS WILLING TO SHOOT ME IF I TRY TO LEAVE THE STADIUM.
THAT'S ENTERTAINMENT.
VERY WELL.
LET'S PUT SOME BEHINDS IN THE SEATS.
KILL IT! KILL IT!
MAKE A WISH, TWO-LEG!

IT'S NOTHING PERSONAL.
WE'LL NOT *ENTIRELY* SO, IN ANY CASE.

A.
AS I'D HOPED. STRONG, BUT NOT THE REAL THING.

LIKE SO MUCH ELSE IN THIS HELLISH PRODUCTION.
STRAIGHT TO VIDEO, NO DOUBT.
QUEEN TSARITSA!
I SAY THAT EACH MELODRAMA NEEDS ITS CLIMAX.
I CHALLENGE YOU.

HM. WHAT GAVE ME AWAY?
BECAUSE YOUR EGO WOULDN'T LET YOU GIVE SOMEONE ELSE THE BEST SEAT IN THE HOUSE, WITCH.

FINE. YOU MAY SUFFER A LIFELESS PAIN, JUST LIKE THE FIRST TIME I MADE SNOW WHITE MY VICTIM.
YES.
WELL, THERE IS ONE DIFFERENCE, THIS TIME.

SNOW WHITE WASN'T TRAINED IN AMBIDEXTROUS DUAL AXE TECHNIQUE!
AND NOW I DO SOMETHING I'VE WANTED TO D SINCE I FIRST SA CINDERELLA.
AAAAIIIIEEEE!!
MURDER YOU! I SWEAR TO STORIES, I WILL FEED YOU IN PIECES TO THREE SEPARATE BEARS!
SHE IS INCALCULABL POWERFUL. BUT S CHOSE THE WRON VENUE.
KILL YOU EAT YOUR FLESH MARRY YOUR FATHER MAKE YOU LOVE MY HATE FOR YOU FOR A THOUSAND CENTURIES!
UHHN!
BECAUSE WE ARE NOW IN AN ARENA.
AND IN ANY ARE REAL OR IMAGINE
I DON'T MUCH LIKE YOUR MANNER, QUEEN.
LET'S HAVE THIS FIGHT MY WAY.

I AM INVINCIBLE!
GHHAAAH!
KILL HER! SHOO... SHOOOOT HER!
WITH WHAT, OH QUEEN? WHAT SHALL THEY SHOOT ME WITH?
DID YOU MEAN WITH THESE ARROWS?
BECAUSE YOU SEE, THAT'S SOMETHING ELSE SNOW WHITE DIDN'T HAVE.
SUPER-SPEED.
YOU'VE BLINDED ME!
YOU IGNORANT PEASANT, YOU'VE BLINDED ME!
I'M AFRAID, QUEEN, THAT I HAVE TO GIVE THIS PROJECT...
...THUMBS DOWN.
I'LL DRINK YOUR BLOOD YET, FAKE PRINCESS. I'LL SEE YOUR FRIENDS IN THE OVEN AT THE HOUSE OF SWEETS.
SHE MEANS IT.
AND AS I SAY, I'VE LEARNED TO MY REGRET THAT YOU CAN'T REALLY KILL HER.

BUT YOU CAN SURELY WORK UP A GOOD SWEAT GETTING NEAR.
NOOOOO!
THAT'S A WRAP, TSARITSA.

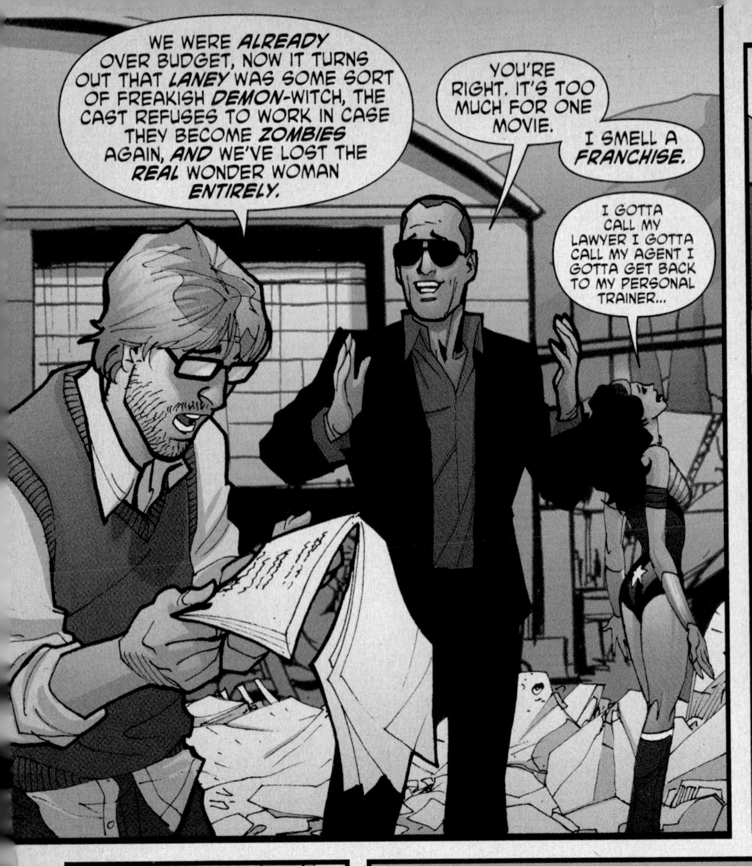
WE WERE ALREADY OVER BUDGET, NOW IT TURNS OUT THAT LANEY WAS SOME SORT OF FREAKISH DEMON-WITCH, THE CAST REFUSES TO WORK IN CASE THEY BECOME ZOMBIES AGAIN, AND WE'VE LOST THE REAL WONDER WOMAN ENTIRELY.
YOU'RE RIGHT. IT'S TOO MUCH FOR ONE MOVIE.
I SMELL A FRANCHISE.
I GOTTA CALL MY LAWYER I GOTTA CALL MY AGENT I GOTTA GET BACK TO MY PERSONAL TRAINER...

THIS "FILM" IS NOTHING BUT A MISHMASH OF BETTER MOVIES AND CYNICAL DISPLAYS OF HUMAN FEMALE FATTY TISSUE.
AND IT LACKS A PROPER SECOND ACT.
NOW FIND THE PRINCESS, OR I WILL TEAR YOU...

SHE EVENTUALLY DISAPPEARED, TO LICK HER WOUNDS, NO DOUBT.
WHICH BROUGHT ME BACK HERE.
WELL, GENTLEMEN.
I'VE DECIDED...

I MUST CONFESS THE ENTIRE PRODUCTION HAS LED ME TO AN EPIPHANY...
....THAT WAITING A WHILE FOR A GOOD MOVIE IS BETTER THAN HAVING A TERRIBLE ONE TODAY.
THIS FILM IS OFFICIALLY ON THE BACK BURNER.

PLEASE FEEL FREE TO DIRECT ALL YOUR ATTORNEYS TO MY ASSOCIATES.
WHERE WE WILL PROMPTLY CONSUME THEM.
WHERE THEY WILL PROMPTLY CONSUME THEM, PRECISELY.

SEVERAL DAYS LATER...
HM.

YOUR MAJESTY.
I THOUGHT YOU MIGHT COME FIND ME.
IT'S "DIANA," PLEASE, MS. CONDERO.

DON'T WORRY. IT'S ICED TEA.
YOU WERE RIGHT.

IT'LL BE ALL RIGHT IF YOU STOP NOW.
WHAT?

HOW DID YOU KNOW, DIANA?
ABOUT THE DRINKING?

I... HAVE A SENSE ABOUT SECRETS, ALLISON.
COULD I TROUBLE YOU FOR A GLASS OF THAT TEA, PERHAPS?
FLYING MAKES ME THIRSTY.

OF COURSE. PLEASE.

YOU COULD HAVE DESTROYED US ALL WITH A FEW WORDS TO THE PRESS. IT WOULD'VE MEANT THE END OF OUR CAREERS.
WE HAVE A SAYING, MY PEOPLE.
"DON'T KILL IF YOU CAN WOUND, DON'T WOUND IF YOU CAN SUBDUE, DON'T SUBDUE IF YOU CAN PACIFY, AND DON'T RAISE YOUR HAND AT ALL UNTIL YOU'VE FIRST EXTENDED IT."

AFTER THE DIVORCE, MY DIVORCE I MEAN...
I JUST FELT SO LONELY, SO HELPLESS ALL THE TIME.
I DID THE BEST I COULD FOR MEG AND TRACY.
I'M NOT HERE TO JUDGE, ALLISON. WE'RE KIND OF BIG ON FREE WILL.
UNTIL THE INNOCENT SUFFER.

THIS IS ADORABLE, BY THE WAY.
Wonder Woman
by Meg age 6
I'M NOT EXCUSING MYSELF. IT'S THE GIRLS. THEY BOTH IDOLIZE YOU.

I SUPPOSE I RESENTED IT.
I MEAN, I SLEEP FOUR HOURS A NIGHT AND STILL GET UP AND MAKE THEIR LUNCHES, PB&J WITH NO CRUSTS.
I GUESS I COULD DO WITH THEM IDOLIZING *ME*, FOR A CHANGE.

MM.
THE WORD "IDOLIZE." ITS ROOTS ARE IN EGYPT.
IT'S NOT ALTOGETHER A PLEASANT CONCEPT, REALLY.

DIANA, I KNOW THE GOOD YOU DO, ALL THE THINGS YOU'VE DONE TO HELP PEOPLE.
I'M SORRY IF I...I'M SORRY FOR HOW I TREATED...
ALLISON.
STOP.

FORGIVEN AND FORGOTTEN.
AND SOME LITTLE GOOD MAY COME OUT OF IT, YES?

DON'T CRY, SISTER.
I'M NOT. NOT REALLY. I'M HAPPY.
BUT...
WHAT DO I DO ON THE NIGHTS WHERE I DON'T HAVE AN AMAZON VISITOR TO KEEP ME HONEST?

THEN I GUESS YOU FIND THE AMAZON THAT WILL NEVER LEAVE YOU.

I BROUGHT BRACERS FOR THE GIRLS. I'LL JUST LEAVE THEM, IF THAT'S...
OH, NO YOU DON'T. IF THEY KNEW YOU'D BEEN HERE AND I DIDN'T WAKE THEM UP, THERE'D BE A RIOT IN THE CONDERO HOUSE.
BUT IT'S A SCHOOL NIGHT...?
WELL, TONIGHT I WON'T MAYBE BE THE MOST RESPONSIBLE MOTHER...

...BUT I'LL CERTAINLY BE THE MOST POPULAR.

WONDER WOMAN!

HELLO, GIRLS. I'M JUST HERE TO VISIT YOUR MOM FOR A MOMENT AND THOUGHT I'D SAY HELLO.
OHMY GODOHMY GODOHMY GODOHMY GOD
CAN WE, CAN WE TAKE A PICTURE? MY *FRIENDS!*
OH, I THINK WE COULD MANAGE *THAT,* IF YOUR MOTHER DOESN'T MIND, OF COURSE?
NO. I DON'T MIND AT ALL.
AND DIANA?

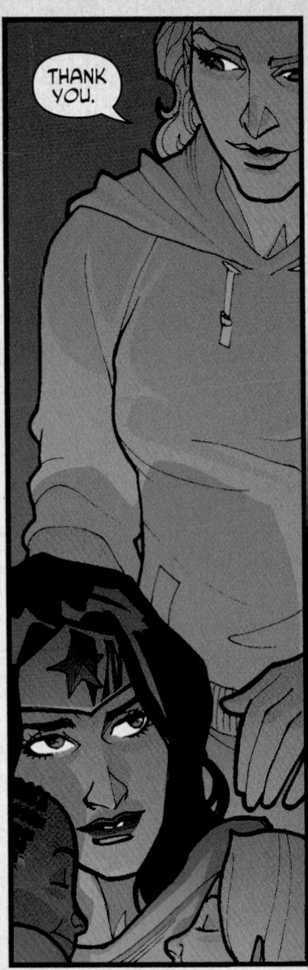
THANK YOU.

CHILDREN.

THEIR JOY IS SO INFECTIOUS, THEY LAUGH COMPLETELY WITHOUT RESERVE.

MY LIFE IS CHANGING SO MUCH LATELY. I CAN IMAGINE THINGS DUTY WOULD NOT ALLOW, PREVIOUSLY.

CHILDREN.

I WONDER.